THE DRAMA SCENE IN NIGERIA

I0576897

Meki Zewi

Cultural & Theatre Arts Consultant.
University of Nigeria. Nsukka.

First Published 2002 by
FOURTH DIMENSION PUBLISHING CO., LTD
16 Fifth Avenue, City Layout. PMB. 01164, Enugu, Nigeria.
Tel+234-42-459969. Fax+234-42-456904.
Email: info@fdpbooks.com, fdpbooks@aol.com
Website: http://www.fdpbooks.com

ISBN 978-156-509-8

CONDITIONS OF SALE

Design and Typesetting by
Fourth Dimension Publishers, Enugu

Dedication

To my father, Daniel Chukwumezie Nzewi, a disciplined disciplinarian who died that peace and love may reign; a dedicated and principled pioneer educationist who had confidence that I would succeed in an unpopular modem profession — music and drama.

Table Of Contents

Introduction

The modern theatre arts disciplines of music, drama and dance are comparatively new fields of academic endeavour in Nigeria. They are fields of study which are just beginning to gain acceptance in the Nigerian's vision of advanced specialist education. The skepticism with which these disciplines were first received as possible areas of academic specialisation arose from the traditional attitude of most Nigerian ethnic societies towards the practice of the creative and performing arts. This traditional attitude was that a person should not perform music, drama or dance as a full-time occupation but rather as an occasional part-time fulfilment of a special genius with which he had been endowed. In fact, in some Nigerian ethnic groups, traditional professional musicians, dramatists and dances were regarded as hirelings, social misfits or as belonging to the lower social class.

With the coming of modem education, music, drama and dance were introduced into school activities first as extra-curricular programmes, then as optional subjects in schools that have an interested master. In the last two decades, music and drama have emerged as school subjects in post primary institutions and are fast gaining ground as independent departments in institutions of higher learning. In fact it can be said that there is a sudden explosion of interest in the study of literary music and drama in Nigeria. Unfortunately, the teaching of these disciplines in schools, colleges and universities has been modelled on the Euro-American practices. There are, as yet, hardly any textbooks or general reading which have attempted to integrate Nigeria's rich and varied traditional theatre practices with the foreign, modem models.

It is the need for African-oriented approach to the study of these artistic disciplines that has prompted the writing of this book. The objective is to emphasize that in our pursuit of modem systems of education and living we need to provide reading texts that will meet up with the modem trends and practices at the same time as they take strong cognizance of our traditional and contemporary models.

The Drama Scene in Nigeria is designed to help aspiring amateurs and professional dramatists as well as drama students in secondary and post secondary institutions in Africa.

Chapter 1

The Drama Scene In Nigeria

Background

There is a heritage of drama and theatre in African cultural traditions. We can define drama as a theatrical display which tells a story or develops a familiar theme or idea using stylized movements, costumes and sound. Theatre is an artistic presentation which offers audio-visual entertainment through stylized movements, costumes and sounds. Although drama is a specialised aspect of the theatre family of artistic presentations, theatre does not necessarily need to have a recognisable story line. Other specialised departments of theatre include music, dance and plastic arts. The word theatre (which not only connotes an artistic performance but is also the name of the venue, especially the building, for such performances) is also synonymous with drama because drama often incorporates music dance, plastic arts and costume.

There are some fundamental distinctions between our traditional drama and literary drama:

1. Literary drama is written drama, while traditional drama is not in written form although through repetition it could acquire a model form and features

2. Literary drama is the creation of one or two writers. Traditional drama is formulated as a group creation, group elaboration of a theme or plot. It is therefore the property of a group or a society.

3. Literary drama uses plots chosen and developed by the writer. This could be fictional or based on real life situations or experiences. The origins and plots of most traditional drama are historical, religious, mythological or topical. The authorship is mostly anonymous.

4. Traditional drama uses common-knowledge backgrounds, themes and references. The dramatic content of a

performance, with respect to plot and story developments, is assumed. The structure therefore tends to be loose. The story line is not always emphasized in dialogue, rather it is commonly denoted in the symbolic features of form and presentation. The structural form of literary drama is concise and the audience requires details of background and development of story line to understand a play as a story. Traditional drama is therefore relevant within a defined social and cultural environment while literary drama is relevant to a more universal audience. For the same reasons, thematic development is often disjointed and diffuse in traditional drama, but more cohesive in literary drama.

5. There is a defined division between performance and audience areas (acting area and audience area) in literary drama. In traditional drama such a division is not very distinct. Quite often the spectators active participation is essential for the realisation of a play.

6. Traditional drama is primarily utilitarian drama. In literary drama utility is subsumed in the entertainment objective and style.

Literary Drama

Literary drama exists side by side with traditional drama in contemporary Africa. Unfortunately as a result of the disruptive influences of modern development which include those of urbanisation, modern education, economic pressures, communication systems and government as well as foreign religion, traditional theatre is no longer as popular with our generation as it was with our ancestors. Nevertheless, traditional drama as part of traditional theatre still commands followership when it is exhibited during certain festival and ritual celebrations that have not died off or been stopped.

Even then the nature of the performances continues to change in attempts to conform with the changing trends in society and government. New forms of indigenous theatre are evolving which boast little of the original socio-political, mystical and ritual effectiveness that made traditional theatre a utilitarian as well as an entertainment establishment for our forefathers. In most instances the dramatized stories or themes have been dropped, omitted or simply forgotten while the superficial and celebrative aspects are abstracted and observed as mere commemorations.

Our first contact with literary drama came in the wake of Western style of education as a component of the study of English language and literature. A name like Shakespeare has come to be well known to the contemporary crop of literate Nigerians who may not boast any knowledge of any accomplished practitioner of traditional theatre arts in their respective villages or communities. But that is the inevitable fate of the oral genre in a transitional literate society. The more reason why there is need for the study of African literary drama which has been influenced by the disappearing traditional sources and styles.

Play acting in post primary institutions started as supports to the study of plays recommended as part of the English literature textbooks. School plays constituted the work (often excerpts of works) of Shakespeare, Goldsmith, Sherridan and a few other popular English playwrights. Occasionally teachers of English language and literature who nurtured love for the stage produced one or two plays not necessarily part of the school text. It is encouraging to note that they never lacked enthusiastic student actors[1] most of whom still boast of their accomplishments as school/college actors.

We have now come to the stage of African plays by African authors. There are now published plays by African authors. And we feel it is relevant to mention a few of these pioneer African playwrights and examples of their published plays:

---

[1] The term actor's as will be used in this book has no sexual discrimination. An actor could therefore be a male or female.

Wole Soyinka: *"The Trial offIrotherJero," "The Lion and the Jewel," "The Road" "Kongi's Harvest"*

John Pepper Clark: *"Song of a Goat," "Ozidi"*

Ola Rotimi: *"Kurunmi," "The gods are not to Blame"*

Zulu Sofola: *"The Wedlock of the Gods," "The Wizard of Law"*

James Ene Henshaw: *"Dinner for Promotion," "Medicine for Love," This is Our Chance"*

Wale Ogunyemi: *"Ijaye War," "Eshu Elegbara"*

J.C. DeGraft: *"Through a Film Darkly" "Sons and Daughters"*

Efua Sutherland: *"Edufa"*

Tsegaye Gabre-Medhiu: *"Oda Oak Oracle"*

Menghista Lemma: *"The Marriage of Unequals'*

Lewis Nkosi: *"The Rhythm of Violence"*

D.D. Phizi: *The Chiefs Bride"*

Olu Olagoke: *"The Incorruptible Judge"*

Sacka Acquaye: *"Obadzeng Goes to Town"*

Meki Zewi: *"Two Fists in One Mouth," "The Lost Finger"*

In the absence of established drama curriculum for schools, most of the available plays do not deliberately aim at school audiences or actors as such. Many are intended for adult audiences while some others offer nothing stimulating to school actors or audiences. A few, however, although not necessarily intended for schools, offer adequate theatre practice and dramatic interest to school drama enthusiasts. A survey did show that most schools were prepared to tackle any available play of African origin whether made up by the drama club masters themselves, or works intended for more experienced theatre practitioners. The results have been mostly either mediocre, or a mockery of the playwrights' ideals.

Written drama, more often than not, requires a special venue with a specified stage (acting area) for the actors. The type of stage for drama presentations has been undergoing changes as dictated by the conceptual developments in the various periods of drama history. The Greeks and Romans used versions of the arena type of theatre. Medieval drama called for mobile platform stage. The Renaissance period (during which Shakespeare lived and wrote) used an apron stage type often with balconies, or a fixed platform stage. The modem period developed the proscenium stage which can also be described as a "picture frame" stage.

The common feature of all these various types of stages is that they were conceived as specially designed enclosures (open air or covered), in which the audience was separated, no matter how distantly, from the actors. There was therefore a demarcation between the audience area of the venue and the acting area. And the name "theatre" was used to identify the entire enclosure. The only possible exception would be the medieval mobile platform stage type. Comparable to the contemporary "theatre on wheels" the medieval mobile stage had acting platforms attached to coaches, but had no special acting enclosures or locations as such. The audience gathered, standing, to watch the travelling theatre in any open ground or public square where the team halted their coaches to give a show.

Literary drama has fixed dialogue which is required to be spoken as written except where a director decides to make some cuts or modifications.

Apart from specifying costumes, literary drama also prescribes locations and properties which are designed and built specially as scene sets for each play, and fixed in the acting area.

Literary drama especially as from the 18th century is usually performed at night when special lighting is used to create moods and to illuminate the visual effects implied or specified in a play. Special sound effects are also exploited. As a matter of fact, stage fighting has now become a specialised branch of lighting technology which produces lamps, bulbs, control board and light effects specially designed for use in theatre performances.

Actors in literary drama could be professionals (who earn their living thereby) or amateurs (who have other employments but act because of their love of acting). Literary drama discriminated against women actors at the early period of its history. From the classical Greek to the late Renaissance periods female parts were acted by young boys or men costumed like women as was done in most of our serious traditional theatre. Now (as also in some aspects of our traditional theatre such as performance on drums previously tabooed to women), it is preferred that female parts be played by female actors while male parts should be taken by male actors. There is nothing wrong however with sex impersonation especially in school plays produced in all male or all female institutions.

Traditional Drama

Traditional festival drama takes place in the open: in the village square, in ritual locations, in the chiefs courtyard, or in a host's compound area. The audience usually encloses the actors in the middle of the "elastic" arena. The actors make their entrances and exits either through the audience or from, and into the shrines, huts or other similar scheduled enclosures that serve the purpose of "preparation rooms." They perform on the same level (ground level) as the audience. Or some members of the audience occupy raised sitting areas enclosing the actors at the lowest level of a bowl-like arrangement.

Quite often the actors involve the audience in their performances by bringing members of the audience into the performance area; or by carrying the action right into the audience; or by exchanging incidental dialogue or dramatic activity with the audience; or by taking their cues for the development of a theme/plot/action or story line from the reactions of the audience. However, the extent to which the audience is involved as participants in traditional drama depends on the category of the drama. For instance, an esoteric drama (i.e. the occult or mystical type that is not open to general public view), or ritual drama (which is utilitarian and psychological drama designed to sustain beliefs by exciting special mystical atmospheres), do not allow random audience participation. Social types on the other hand, which are conceived as public information and education, social commentaries, corrective satires, topical caricatures, ancestral or spiritual communions as well as morality play types would not be successful presentations without active audience participation.

Traditional drama calls for special functional costumery which give visual, symbolic and psychological effectiveness to the performances. Some types, again the ritual and esoteric types, prefer ancient costumes which were believed to posses certain mystical potency enhanced by age. The more social types continue to modify and upgrade their costumes to reflect the times.

Traditional social drama takes place either during day time, or in the moonlight. Small audience types that could take place in courtyards require the illumination from an intimate bonfire or vegetable torches. Esoteric types could take place during dark nights when they involve a non-seeing ethnic audience; or in the moonlight, or with bonfire and torch illuminations in special location for the initiated.

Sound effects as well as magical effects are used to enhance the mood and atmosphere of the performances. For instance, the sound of animals which feature in traditional drama are usually mechanically simulated. Magical effects help to sustain the myth and potency which are implied or manifested in traditional drama.

Traditional drama requires talented and accomplished actors who are often required to undergo periods of training and apprenticeship. They mature from minor roles to principal roles. In some occult types the artistes are camped and placed under certain taboos in order to ensure proper mental and physical conditioning for a successful performance. Except in isolated instances, women axe not allowed to act in traditional drama. Female roles are played by costumed male actors. But traditional actors, although accomplished artists, are not always professionals;

Our study of drama will tend to stress the merits of literary drama which, apart from its other values in general education, prepares gifted students for more serious professional or amateur careers in the creative, cultural and performing arts disciplines. It is important in the process to recognize the merits of our traditional drama especially since some of our contemporary African playwrights as well as the theatre establishments of the Western world draw their inspiration and materials from traditional African sources and styles. Tradition-inspired plays by African authors have prescribed modem theatre techniques and technology in efforts to give greater effectiveness to our traditional forms and styles. The extent to which these are desirable or have been successful is not our concern here. Drama as a creative discipline must reflect the life, environment and living circumstances of its practitioners.

The Artist in Nigeria Society

One of the inhibiting factors for prospective Nigerian actors, and indeed modern actors in most other African societies, has been that of social acceptability. A cross section of the Nigerian society, for instance tends to regard people who go on stage as unconventional people. Artists (whether painters, sculptors, musicians, carvers, dancers, dramatists, actors) are not "crazy" people. In our traditional heritage, performing artists such as musicians, carvers, dancers, dramatists actors, were very much respected in the socio-political milieu. They were the mirror of the society as well as the watch dogs of social ethics and mores. They, as citizens, therefore maintained exemplary standards of respectability. In recognition of their artistic talents and their role in some traditional societies, they were looked upon as celebrities — people of a higher social stratum entitled to some uncommon social and political privileges. Most traditional creative and performing artistes were people who had other subsistence occupation like every other citizen. They practised their arts as special accomplishments. We refer to them as professionals with respect only to their artistic proficiency. Those who depended on the remunerations from their practices for their livelihood, i.e. subsistence professionals, although respected for their accomplishments, did not enjoy the same high social prestige as those who had other livelihood occupations.

At the early stages of Nigerian exposure to the modern brand of civilization, a new type of professional performing artiste emerged in the form of the night club music entertainer. A majority of these musicians were social drop-outs with little education who drifted into the urban areas to grab a cheap living. They became social misfits because of their low morals as well as their irresponsible and reckless social behaviour. Consequently they were snubbed, exploited and denigrated by the society who, nevertheless, patronized their music. These bad eggs of the theatre profession lived from hand to mouth and gave the performing arts profession rather low reputation and rating in the modern Nigerian society. On the other hand, elsewhere in the more technologically advanced societies, performing artistes, were rated at the very top of the social strata, economic stature, and celebrity rating. They are social idols.

Happily, more and more people in our modem society are beginning to realise that the night club musician does not in any way represent the modern concept and practice of professionalism in the creative and performing arts. Even a few of the night club artistes themselves are remodeling their social image and life styles and are gaining social and economic recognition.

A new body of professionals is beginning to emerge in the visual arts, music, drama and dance. These are well educated trained and responsible practitioners who are conscious of the values and virtues of their professions, and whose names are accordingly celebrated in our social circles. Their works and lives are examples of achievement which are very much discussed and quoted at home and abroad. As the creative, cultural, and performing arts professions produce exemplary human successes, the importance of these professions in a balanced and progressive society is gaining merited recognition in educational and other national planning. The study of these professional disciplines which was previously ignored is now being emphasized in our educational systems. For instance in the Nigerian universities and most other post-secondary institutions there are now special departments that offer diploma, graduate and post-graduate studies in plastic and applied arts, music, drama, dance and theatre studies generally. These departments are gradually producing a core of academicians, teachers and practitioners in these various professions. Some others are receiving their studies and apprenticeship in overseas institutions and establishments. In post-primary institutions, increasing attention is being paid to courses in these fields in order to encourage among the students an awareness of their importance to the overall mental and academic preparation of a man in society. Planners of education are now becoming concerned about achieving balanced general education at the base relevant to our cultural situation.

Problem of Facilities

The problems facing developing nations with respect to modem educational facilities cannot be solved overnight. An awareness of such problems is, however, important. A solution would be magnificent. But the lack of the most modern facilities should in no way discourage the pursuance of our goals. What is most desirable is that we demonstrate an investigative spirit; improvise and experiment with, and adapt, the facilities available in our own environment to achieve our goals. That excites our creative ingenuity and gives us originality. In the long run our achievements would even be seen to be none the worse for the absence of ready made and imported techniques and technology. What must be encouraged in our students, especially in the creative and performing arts, is an innovative and experimental attitude of mind. Inadequacies within our most modem communication systems and facilities, for instance, have not stopped people from accomplishing their communication and economic objectives. So be it with drama courses and play production in our schools.

Our forefathers achieved high artistic standards of performance and presentation with available local technological facilities. They adapted the resources of their environment to evolve their production techniques. A play could be performed anywhere at anytime. What matters is that the artistic-aesthetic standard of production and presentation should be worth the while of the audience. Any play could be adapted to any available production and performance situation. As long as we have open air and dry weather, as well as an acting area and audience area on different levels, there are basic facilities for play production. We do not have to plead lack of a theatre hail or lighting facilities. A matinee performance would do. What might be lacking would be an imaginative and competent director/producer and/or enthusiastic student actors.

In the contemporary Nigerian theatre scene most performing troupes who are of advanced artistic status like the Theatre Company of the University of Ife, the Drama Company of the Theatre Arts Department of the University of Ibadan, The Anaedo Production 4-D and die Oak Theatre both of the University of Nigeria, Nsukka are all experimenting more and more with open air performances. As a matter of fact, the defunct On Olokun Theatre of the University of Ife was essentially an open air theatre located in the ancient town of Ile-Ife. The concept of the theatre was derived from traditional models. Modem features were designed into it in order to suit and reflect our contemporary visions.

It must be understood when we talk of traditional styles that our forefathers exploited all resources available at every given stage of their cultural evolution to the best advantage. As their ingenuity improved their environment and material technological resources, their styles of life and artistic expressions were modified to incorporate the advantages of the new trends or discoveries. At the same time they were never shy of borrowing and incorporating whatever was progressive and essential from other cultures that they had contact with. We are, therefore, not advocating that what is best for us should be what was best for our ancestors while what is wrong for us is what is foreign to our tradition. Rather we are saying that we will welcome what is useful in the foreign, and adapt or integrate it into our resources. That way we will still have the pride of cultural identity, as well as of original thinking not only in the concept and style, but also in the development of our artistic creativity and presentations.

The Actor and His Audience

Our traditional background of audience attitudes seems to have influenced our present day theatre audience whose behaviour differs from that of theatre audiences in the Western world. Theatre history records, however, that there were periods in Western drama when audiences exhibited comparable mannerisms and attitudes as are now found in our society.

It is important for anybody going on the modern stage to know something about the audience behaviour that he/she may have to confront. This will help the actors maintain their composure on stage, and time their dialogues and actions to the best advantage of a presentation. Such a knowledge will also help the play director in the training of his actors and in styling the production of any given play. To be ignorant of one's audience is like adventuring into a grisly dark forest without taking adequate precautions.

A summary of the typical attitudes of Western modern theatre audiences would be helpful in understanding our own contemporary theatre audience. There is now a tradition in Western theatre practice of media criticism. That is, there is a group of people called theatre critics who are supposed to be critically perceptive in the arts of writing for the theatre, theatre production and presentation. These critics undertake to preview theatre productions, assess the quality of the material and its interpretation and, publish their judgment of its worth in the popular newspapers, magazines and other public information media. These critics now greatly influence the attitude of Western theatre audiences, and to a great extent determine the success or failure of a play, film, and other artistic exhibitions or performances. A majority of the Western theatre audience depends on the opinions of these critics to guide them in choosing what performances will be worth their investment. Their attendance, in addition, is in itself a clue to how they appreciate the show. Having now decided to watch a performance, the Western theatre audience is expected to conduct itself with formal decorum during the show. The couple next to you also paid good money. Therefore you must respect their feelings - their right to undisturbed appreciation of the show. You must be restrained in your applauses, disapproval and other emotional, vocal, or behavioral responses to whatever is happening on stage. Contrarily, the Nigerian theatre goer, when expressing his reactions to a performance, tends to have little or no consideration for the feelings of his/her neighbours. For the Western audience it is extreme bad manners if someone's responses to any aspect of a production constitutes a marked disturbance or distraction to the actors. Such a person would be said to be ill-bred, uncultured and uncivilized. One is not even expected to stand or move about while a performance is going on. There is usually an intermission (for longer shows) when members of the audience can ease or stretch themselves or take refreshments before watching the concluding half of the presentation. And anybody who, out of boredom or any other reasons, does not wish to continue watching the show could seize that opportunity to go away. If after watching a show one has any further reason to make public his/her appreciation or disapproval of the show or any aspect of it, such a person does so by sending his/her comments to the newspapers, magazines or journal for publication. Or he/she could write straight to the producer/director, artist or actor concerned.

It should be added here that the above is now regarded as the ideal modern audience attitude. The new generation of Western theatre audience, i.e. the youths of the Western countries, are becoming erratic and unrestrained in their emotional exhibitions during theatre presentations especially "pop" theatre shows pop music concerts. They have even been known to heckle, boo and throw rubbish on artists during performances they disapprove of; while distracting those they approve of with their enthusiastic feet stamping, yodelling and wild acclamations. The irresponsible behaviour of this new generation of Western audience has even been extended to the destruction of property and such other riotous wildness. In short there is now a disquieting tendency for the younger generation in Western theatre audiences to constitute a nuisance to the artistes on stage as well as to other more disciplined members of the audience. It is only fair however to mitigate this assessment by observing that most of the artistes, especially the "pop" music artists, tend to measure their success and acceptability by the degree of wildness or uproar with which their performances are received.

It must be noted that the attitude of an audience is greatly influenced by the physical nature of the performance venue. That is to say, the physical relationship between the audience and the performers within a given venue inclusive of the degree to which the performers involve the audience in their style of presentation. Where an audience is effectively separated from the performers there is a greater tendency for the audience to be more restrained in their attitude towards the actors and their performance. The other situation is where the audience is in close contact or at the same level with the performers. The performers move in and Out of the audience, or provoke one form of physical interaction with them or another, and thereby involve them in the performance business. Given such a close physical relationship, the audience cannot help being a participant-audience. As a matter of fact in our traditional styles of presentation, dialogue plays rather a secondary role in drama presentations for large audiences. The story was often symbolized and communicated through mime, dance and costume. Dialogue when employed was directed at only a small section of the audience at a time. Such localised verbal exchange would not necessarily promote the unfolding of the plot. Quite often they would be extemporised sidelines intended to cheer, or erupt expressed responses for the benefit of that section of the audience to which they were addressed. This type of audience relationship would not be ideal for the presentation of literary drama which depends primarily on dialogue or speech to deliver its goods. Thus even in our advocacy for traditionally inspired literary drama, a raised performance stage or contrarily, a raised audience section, at least, would be more ideal for a meaningful presentation. There should be an appreciable physical demarcation between the acting area and the audience area that would help to curb the inherent participant urges of our audience. Unless the production demands otherwise, anything that undermines the effectiveness of the spoken word in literary drama is not good for the modern theatre in Africa or elsewhere.

In effect then, the traditional audience is a participant-audience that necessitates greater reliance on mime, costume and dance than on dialogue for dramatic exposition. This is not to say that there are no traditional drama types that are dependent on the spoken word. For such types of drama, movement, costume and mime were still essential elements, and although the physical relationship between actors and the audience remained fluid the audience realised that they were dependent primarily on the spoken word to appreciate a presentation.

The modern Nigerian audience, that is, the type found in the urban centres and schools, is not yet emotionally emancipated from its traditional audience heritage. Lack of adequate performance venue has contributed to this. Nigeria can only boast of a few theatres ideal for drama presentations. In other instances where halls (school assembly halls or town halls not really designed for play presentations) and, at times, raised platforms are available, physical demarcation between audience and performers are inadequate. Not only that, seating arrangements might be insufficient and uncomfortable, and there could be inadequate entrances and exits for both performers and audience. Whenever the audience and performances share the same exits and entrances there are bound to be distractions and disturbances. In a hail where the seating arrangement is not on bleachers and the stage not sufficiently raised, spectators are bound to stand up, sit up, shift and shuffle quite often in an attempt to secure more advantageous views of the activities on stage.

A characteristic of our modern theatre audience which has been mentioned in passing earlier is the lack of consideration for the feelings of others in the audience. During a performance, spectators freely engage in loud private dialogues and side repartee within the hall. They shout, laugh loudly, heckle, yell and whisper their comments or commentaries without consideration for the views or interests of their neighbours who are intent on following and understanding what the actors are saying.

Part of the problem with the modem Nigerian theatre scene is that literary drama has been stripped of the mysteries and psychological effects of the traditional theatre which conditioned its audience. This disenchantment was effected by the discrediting and exorcist methods of foreign religion and its allies: modem education modem technology and its wares, as well as the scientific maxim of "seeing is believing." So the traditional myths and values sustained by faith and trust have been undermined and eroded. The modern Nigerian audience has thus become skeptical about the methods and values of drama as well as about the role of actors. In the process of this alienation from the implications and effect of traditional drama we find that the Nigerian audience has equally been purged of the vital sensitivity to emotional truths of drama. Thus, whereas a traditional audience would exhibit empathy with the emotions of performers and the credibility of their acting, the contemporary audience is often detached from the emotions communicated and exhibited by the actors. They insensitively laugh where they ought to feel pity, for instance. With the same detachment, they openly shout their challenges, agreement, support or other rejoinders often deliberately intended to distract or embarrass the actors on stage. A traditional audience would only volunteer such interjections at the instance of a performer who needed it as a cue or lead-on for further development of the dramatic event. A Western ideal audience is not expected to offer audible comments or rejoinders during a performance.

Where the quality of the performance has been exceptionally good, a certain cross section of the modern Nigerian audience has been noted however, to exhibit ideal audience attitudes. There are now signs of a growing trend towards an ideal audience attitude with what could be called the enlightened section of our audiences. At the middle and low-brow levels the mental attitude which sees a drama presentation as mere entertainment with no spiritual or socio-political messages still persists.

As a work of art a play should edify its audience. To be edified the audience needs to be contemplative instead of merely emotional. A play is dramatised story of a human situation which therefore has such relevant implications as: its moral value, its character study, its situational analysis of a society and its people's behaviour, its exposition of social, political or religious trends, its spiritual sustenance as an aesthetic and artistic creation. If these qualities are present and are effectively portrayed in production and presentation, an audience needs to be sensitive to them while in the process enjoying the other equally very vital quality of drama as entertainment. Good playwrights like some other artists are psychics, with acute sensitivity to their environment. They are, therefore, often social commentators. It is disturbing when in a formative society like ours these implications woven into the plays by our playwrights (who are sensitive) are lost on the society because it has constituted itself into an uncontemplative and uncommitted audience. Quite often one assesses our audiences as, in effect, gobbling the entertainment thrills of a play while wishing back the implied message on the writer and the actors. On the other hand it is only fair to observe that some of our playwrights (published and unpublished) have nothing of value to say to humanity apart from vague and often slapstick entertainment drama. If a play has nothing of spiritual or intellectual value to offer its audience other than sensational thrills, how can the emerging audience be helped to appreciate the true value of drama? Again there is lacking an impressive supply of sensitive actors. If a message is poorly delivered, the audience will be expected to laugh off its message. It is therefore important to lay a foundation of good plays, and at the same time encourage capable and talented actors, in order to mould an ideal audience which can sustain a theatre industry.

It is unfortunate that the present attitude of our audience has affected the off-stage relationship between actors and the audience i.e., the society. It has made the society look at stage artists not as gifted and skilled interpreters of a role, but rather as people who are exhibiting their personal lives on stage. Some narrow-minded parents therefore strongly discourage their children, especially daughters, from taking part in plays or even ever dreaming about a career on stage where their talents would be most rewardingly applied. The society, instead of introspective identification with the characters being impersonated by actors, prefer to brand the actors with the roles they depict on stage. This is an unfortunate attitude which makes the actors vicarious scape-goats. In real fact, the actor on stage is portraying not his/her character but is rather a mirror reflecting the playwright's impressions about the lives and character traits (virtuous or atrocious) of his society which includes members of the audience.

This audience attitude has so far inhibited the blossoming of virile theatre in Nigeria by dampening the latent urge to go on stage felt by those who have the talent or feel a call to pursue a career in theatre. The following anecdote will help to illustrate the unfortunate attitudes of our so-called enlightened" older generation which have so far discouraged the emancipation of theatre movement in our society.

Once in a Nigerian University the members of staff felt a need to start a drama club in order to enliven their social environment. A call was put out by the conveners and there was an enthusiastic response from staff and wives of staff. A meeting was accordingly held to cast the club's first play and assign production responsibilities. The play chosen (written by a Ghanaian) involved four female characters. One of these female characters was portrayed in the play as a woman who, as a result of her emotional frustrations, demonstrated questionable social reputation. Another woman was characterised as a prying social nuisance. A third woman was represented as the popular concept of an ideal housewife and woman in society. The first woman character was the principal character in the play. The second woman was another important part while the third woman had a minor role. What transpired in the casting exercise was that none of the housewives (staff wives) agreed to act the first two roles. Infact the two housewives who were tentatively cast in those two roles before the meeting were very cross with the conveners for being so wicked and insinuative as to assign them such "horrible" roles. Every woman member of the club opted for the minor part of the ideal housewife. They openly voiced their preference as being prompted by the fact that the character represented the society's impression of an ideal woman. And although the housewives who were given the principal female roles could easily have carried the parts from the artistic point of view, their reason for rejecting the parts was significant: that their stage roles were assigned to them according to their characters in real life, and would thereby run them down and discredit them in the community. It is not relevant here to go into the maturity of their reasons. What is important is that none of these women (a majority of whom had university degrees or diplomas) consented, after all persuasions and assurances as to the fact that drama is only make-believe. And of course, the play was not performed and the incipient drama club died a worthy, natural death on the spot.

With drama and other disciplines of the creative and performing arts becoming part of the primary and post-primary school curricula, a new generation of audience types who understand the ideals and merits of stage performances as well as a properly oriented crop of talented, trained and enlightened actors will emerge. A healthy environment for drama and dramatists can be created. On this foundation can also be built a progressive, viable and glorious stage industry.

Chapter 2

Drama As A School Subject

Tim Efobi & Ada Eke

I first met Tim Efobi at the University in 1961. He was an engineering student. Tall, barrel-chested and imposingly well built, he had a good voice, and was interested in singing. So he joined the university choir as a lead tenor. During his first year, the Music Department of the University adventured into a production of Verdi's opera "Aida." Tim was given the lead male role, Radamis, which calls for an elastic tenor range. There was no need to rewrite the music to suit Tim because he already had a vibrant natural range of three octaves, although he had never received formal music training, not to talk of any voice training whatsoever.

By the first night of performance it was already obvious that Tim possessed a rare, potential operatic tenor voice. Not only was his natural range wide, but he had a bravura that could subdue a chorus and fill a theatre at forte passages. It was equally melifluous in bel canto melodies. Tim so astounded everybody as a rare talent and a possible asset to the entire operatic world that the lecturer-producers (who were Americans) immediately initiated a move to secure him a place in an American music conservatory where he could formally train as an operatic performer. The Chancellor of the University who was the guest of honour during that first night was so impressed that he lent his support to the arrangement. He offered to help secure a scholarship as soon as a school could be found for Tim. A school was found and arrangements for Tim's travel were set in motion. Tim himself was enthusiastic. He was determined to pursue a stage career and drop engineering.

But alas! when Tim travelled home to inform his family about his good fortune, and to make the final arrangements for

21

his departure to a new life and career in the United States of America a nasty shock awaited him. His people at home confronted him with a stout wall of opposition. To go on stage and jump about singing for a living? Could he compete with the local minstrel who nevertheless, made a comfortable living as a basket maker?

What madness! Oh, he wants to be a lost son? Real madness to drop such a prestigious course as engineering (as exemplified by Mr Butterscotch, the British engineer who made roads and had a car to show for it). And then to drop engineering in favour of a vagabond's life on a modern stage as a singer. Incredible! Did he want to shame his parents? Cause them to join their ancestors precipitatedly? And he, the first son, for that matter. Whoever heard of a responsible man pursuing a career as a public entertainer? Who in their society had ever done it before? People went abroad to become doctors, lawyers and other prestigious professionals. Now that it was their fortune for their son to go abroad on scholarship he said he would be going to do singing and acting. What misfortune! Oh No! He would do that over their dead bodies. And so on...

There was such an outcry that Tim was convinced he was about to commit an abhorable prodigal act. So he backed out of the programme. Everybody in the University connected with arrangements for his travel and study was shattered, especially the expatriates, whites and black, who could not understand the cultural opposition to such a covetable opportunity in Western culture. But there it was. All arrangements were canceled with regrets. And Tim continued with his course in mechanical engineering. He continued however to take interest in stage activities. The following year he starred as King Kong in the South African jazz opera of that name by Todd Matshikiza.

Tim got his first degree making an excellent class in mechanical engineering. He became a brilliant engineer and is established in Lagos. But what most people don't know is that

Tim has continued to cherish a dream of making a brilliant career on stage. He continues to seize any opportunity to go on stage that would not compromise his increasing responsibilities as a top engineering executive.

As self-confident as he was powerfully built, Tim could not easily disregard his family's opposition to his ambition, especially as a first born in his culture. That dream, which, had it materialised may or may not have been of greater benefit and credit to his family, is now receding more and more as his engineering career offers him less and less respite to indulge his artistic talent.

In our traditional society, Tim could have been a celebrity as a performer. But since tradition did not accept proficiency or talent in the artistic fields as a marketable commodity with which to earn full-time livelihood, he could still have been successful in another subsistence occupation as he is now with engineering. In tradition, talent, is a divine endowment and is treated with reverence. It is not to be prostituted for a living, although it can be acknowledged with gifts and praise. Traditionally, therefore, the creative and performing artists were special people. Talents were encouraged from childhood and given special opportunities and training to develop because a celebrated traditional artist was a credit to his family and people generally. But making a living as a performer was frowned upon as a degradation of a divine favour, and such people became near social misfits.

Our contemporary society is facing a cultural imbroglio, trying to forge new value systems from the conflicts of the alien versus the traditional. In the interim, the modern society seems to have just overcome the traditional scorn for subsistence professionalism in the creative and performing arts, and is on the threshold of upholding the traditional recognition and respect for the arts and their practitioners. In the modem milieu this would spell a befitting social status as well as accruing economic boom for the practitioners. If Tim Efobi had been born a couple of decades later with his talents, perhaps, the world would have witnessed an operatic King from Africa.

Ada Eke is a girl from the same Nigerian cultural background as Tim Efobi. Her story started much more recently at a time when we had advanced our modern concepts of life. Her parents belong to the successful, well-educated class that are looked upon as "leaders of thought" both in official and social circles. This does not necessarily imply those who have attained broad-minded vision of life, for most "leaders of thought" are seriously shackled by atavism as well as myopic and narrow-minded views on issues.

After her primary school education, Ada entered one of the most popular secondary schools in the country usually regarded as a privileged school. Ada was both privileged and brilliant. The principal of the school was an expatriate English lady who studied classics and loved the arts, especially music and drama. At a time when the educational authorities and the parents were pressurizing her to pay primary attention to educating their children in the sciences, Miss Dankworth understood the dangers of lopsided exposition in early education. She well understood the long-term advantages of maintaining a balance between the arts and the sciences at the formative secondary school age. So without unduly hurting the feelings and wishes of the powerful class in society and government who wanted all their children to be groomed for future careers in medicine and the sciences, Miss Dankworth maintained a tradition of unofficial courses in music, drama and plastic arts for all students in the lower classes. With tact born of experience (for she was an elderly educationist), Miss Dankworth continued to weather the interference, and kept up her school's reputation in brilliant drama and musical productions. Year by year her school won the lion's share of all the first and second class certificates in music, drama and plastic arts during the annual festival of the arts competitions (The Festival of the Arts was organised and run by a non-government voluntary organisation calling itself the Arts Council).

By her third year at school Ada had already become a prima donna in her school's annual operetta productions, as well as being acclaimed a talented actress. She made prize-winning appearances in competitions, and was in demand for concerts both in the school and in public functions. Her parents viewed her increasing stage popularity with mixed feelings. Friends advised them that encouraging Ada's stage appearances would bring her in contact with men admirers and expose her to corrupt influences. So a cold war ensued between Ada's parents and Miss Dankworth who adamantly encouraged the development of Ada's artistic talents. Ada's parents sent letters to education authorities condemning Miss Dankworth, the Principal, for exposing her students to corrupt influences. They and their cronies lobbied for her removal as the school principal or possibly her dismissal. Ironically the same lobbyists clamoured for front-or special seat reservations during the school's famous annual drama and music night. Such performances were always well attended by dignitaries in government and private sectors including the Minister of Education and quite often the head of government who attended as the guests of honour.

In appropriate circles when it became fashionable, Ada's parents would boast about their daughter's talent~ and glow in the praises attracted by her stage successes. On such occasions they would even banteringly vie for the honour of having passed such artistic talents on to her, genetically.

Miss Dankworth was one of the oldest and most respected Principals in the Ministry of Education, expatriate or no expatriate. So all the groundless petitions and lobbying against her failed to achieve the results wished by her detractors. One of the reasons for this was the fact that the then Chief Inspector of Education was himself a lover of the performing arts. Although a chemistry graduate from Oxford University, the Chief Inspector featured commendably in one or two plays during his undergraduate days and was never tired of regaling his listeners with accounts of his near stage stardom as an undergraduate.

By the time Ada finished her secondary school education she had proved to be an all round brilliant student who topped her class in the sciences as well as in the arts in spite of her constant stage appearances. She came out with her school's best result in grade one in the West African School Certificate result for that year. Her principal, Miss Dankworth, recommended a career in the performing arts for her, and even offered to make contacts in Britain for the best placement that would be of benefit to the development of her artistic promise. But to assert their parental authority over the life and career of their child, the Ekes bundled their daughter, Ada, into a medical school in Britain as soon as they secured an admission for her. And to ensure that she did not follow the "wayward" path of further stage dreams, they commissioned a townsman and his wife who were then resident in that part of Britain to police Ada's private life and interests.

Ada obediently left for Britain and an imposed career in medicine; but not without gratefully collecting helpful addresses and letters of introduction from her mentor, Miss Dankworth, in the event that she could spare time from medicine to take part time music and acting lessons.

Artistry is intoxicating once it is exposed and catches on. The only force that can suppress artistic or creative drive thereafter is lack of opportunity.

So, as soon as Ada settled down in her new environment and medical studies in Britain, she decided to explore Miss Dankworth's contacts. To her joyous amazement she discovered that the good woman had preceded her with glowing recommendations. However, Ada soon proved the tributes of Miss Dankworth and won the admiration of her instructors. It must be said for Ada that although she was exceedingly pretty, with a model's figure and an elegant deportment to match, she was as sensible and humble as she was ambitious. She was never swollen-headed either about her physical graces or her initial successes as a stage talent.

By the end of her second year in Britain Ada found herself a dropout in medicine. This was not as a result of an inability to cope. Rather it was a voluntary decision to pursue a more stimulating career that would give her more sense of personal fulfilment in life. Her grades were good enough by the end of her second year in medicine, but she was already finding the course a drudge. And Ada had a temperament that would not subject itself to compulsive boredom even for the sake of remaining in her parent's good books. At her request, her part-time instructors in music and acting helped her secure a place in a British College of Music and Drama.

Diligently Ada wrote to thank Miss Dankworth for helping her discover herself. She obediently wrote her parents to inform them about her change of career. She also announced to her parents that with the help of her instructors she had secured a scholarship for her new course in music and drama. But Mr Eke would not accommodate such a "disgrace" as having his daughter pursue a career on stage. So, keeping the news secret even from his wife, he started making travel arrangements. Within three weeks of getting Ada's letter, and without giving Ada any advanced warning as to his intentions, Mr Eke arrived in Britain. He sought out Ada in her new institution and proceeded without formalities to bully her. Then, not making much headway in achieving his objective by that method, he resorted to imploring Ada not to disgrace him and his public image by exposing her "decent" and prestigious family background to scorn as a stage artist. Needless to say, Ada's mind was made up to stick to the only career and profession that gave meaning to her life. She mildly but firmly pleaded with her father that she had her own life to live; that she was not interested in merely parading her family background; that she preferred to prove herself with her own God-given qualities; moreover, that a stage career in advanced societies is one of the most coveted and respected professions;

and that only a few aspirants manage to make a breakthrough. She went on to note that; those who are opportuned and who possess the requisite talent and industry to make a success of it are a great pride to their families and country as whole; and that Nigeria required talented and opportuned people like her to stimulate an awareness about the merits and opportunities of the performing arts professions in the country.

But her further efforts at sharing her dreams about the wonderful future that awaited her as one of the pioneer Nigerian stage celebrities were silenced with a threat. Her father vowed to disown her if she defied his wishes and a refused to bow to parental dictation about her life and career. Ada made it clear that she would always cherish and respect her parents, but that at the same time she would prefer to be disowned than to disown herself by being unfaithful to herself and her God-given talents, not to talk of being dishonest about her career ambition.

Thereupon Mr. Eke adamantly disowned his daughter and ordered her to stop associating herself with his "prestigious" name. These far-reaching, reckless decisions he confirmed by letter as soon as he travelled back to Nigeria. Mr. and Mrs. Eke privately mourned their living daughter and nearly burst veins clouting down upon their other children who became jubilant on learning that their sister would soon be one of the celebrated actors and singers whom they were always agog to read about in magazines, and to idolize in films. The children kept a respectful silence over their parents' angry disapproval of any mention of Ada's name in the house. But secretly they vied for the number of letters they sent to Ada as well as the number of copies of photographs of her stage appearances in various roles and productions which she sent to them. These they proudly displayed at special corners of their albums or as pin ups in their dormitory corners at school. Soon Ada's brothers and sisters started to enjoy special attention at school from their mates for being close relations of an up and coming star.

Then to boost the pride of her brothers and sisters, Ada's photograph illuminated the front page of one of Nigeria's leading newspapers. There was a full story in the centre page of the publication about her achievements as a brilliant Nigerian actress in Britain who was also a popular model and a charming television hostess. The story announced that Ada has just won an important part in a feature film, the shooting of which would involve locations in Ghana and possibly Nigeria. The feature write-up was in Ada's stage name, for in obedience to her father's command she had assumed the stage name of Ada Ogali. Ogali was her maternal grandfather's first name, and Ada had enjoyed a warm relationship with her grandfather who had died a year before she left secondary school.

Mr. and Mrs. Eke did not know how to take the sudden celebrity status in Nigeria of their disowned daughter. Neither of them had ever been featured in any newspaper, even if only in a group photograph or the "also were there" mentions. At government parties which they had religiously attended on invitations, press photographers always preferred to release those shots in which, at the luckiest, the sleeve of Mrs. Eke's gorgeous blouses appeared; but never the complete identifying features of either of them. To compound their feelings, telegrams of congratulations started pouring in. Not to talk of telephone calls from enthused well-wishers. Some wrote letters of warm tribute to the Ekes but urged them to persuade their daughter to allow her people to share in her glories by disclosing her proper parentage in future publicities. While Mr. and Mrs. Eke were still busy covering up the embarrassment caused by the congratulatory messages and mentions, newspapers one morning proudly announced the arrival of their daughter Ada, in Nigeria. Apparently the previous write-up on Ada was used by the film company to prepare the Nigerian public for the launching of Ada as the star actress in a film, the shooting of which had been advanced at the time.

Mr. Eke's town's union, Lagos branch, quickly rallied and accorded Ada a much publicised and most lavish heroine's welcome. Various other bodies and even the appropriate government organ participated in giving her a reception, the type of which was usually reserved for visiting stage dignitaries. Enthusiastically, her proud town union arranged a triumphant entry for Ada's visit to her town, the town that produced such a celebrated star. Mr. and Mrs. Eke were overwhelmed by the sequence and speed of events and suddenly found themselves blazoned into unmerited limelight. They were steamrolled into appropriately honourable positions in the reception sponsored by the town for the daughter whom they had disowned. The Ekes were thoroughly ashamed of themselves for their narrow-mindedness and consequent rashness about their daughter's career. But Ada did not give them any chance to feel defeated or deflated. She gave a surprising speech at the reception (which was also her first meeting with her parents since the unfortunate confrontation in Britain). In her speech she laid much emphasis on the moral support of her family. It was their strong encouragement that gave her the courage to pursue such a rare career which was so easily misunderstood in Nigeria, even among the so-called enlightened or educated circles.

At home that night her proud parents humbly welcomed back their daughter and decorously asked for her forgiveness which they knew was granted even before the asking. During that visit, Ada later explained to her brothers and sisters that she wholeheartedly forgave her parents because it was not really their fault. What happened was an unfortunate result of the attitude of the society to which they belonged, and which misunderstood the disciplines and opportunities of her stage profession. Moreover, she said, it was really the stiff parental opposition that made her determined to make a resounding success of the career in order, not only to highlight the merits and opportunities of the profession, but also to pose a star image that would encourage parents of other gifted youngsters to give their children a chance -at least to a free choice of career.

Ada is now married. She is still achieving more honours on stage. She is now a celebrated television personality and has starred in three feature films. She and her husband, who studied the plastic arts, are planning to return and settle down in Nigeria. They arc looking forward to lending their experiences and expertise to the federal and state governments' efforts to establish and encourage professional theatres. They are convinced that there is now a strong foundation and persuasion for the establishment of professional performing arts movement in Nigeria.

Ada is quite wealthy as a result of her stage contract earnings. Although much more popular than her husband, such popularity has not changed her fundamental humility. She has a happy family and devotes her time after rehearsals and performances to her husband and their two children - a boy and a girl. Her family is always in the front row during the first night of every new show she takes part in. Her husband, Udoka, is proud of her stage career and stage success. He adores Ada because she is a homely and adorable housewife. Her husband had spent the past three years doing his post-graduate specialisation and apprenticeship as a stage designer. Now that he has finished and acquired working experience in British theatres, they have decided that they would best serve their professions in Nigeria. Their return will no doubt give a big boost to the development of the creative and performing arts professions in Nigeria. And no doubt Ada will be an invaluable encouragement to gifted boys and girls and who are looking forward to an acting career. There is opportunity now to start early and there is a golden future awaiting those who have the talent and ambition that makes stage and film stars.

Why Do We Study Drama?

The question still arises: Why do we study drama? Why should we study drama if only the so-called talented have the possibility of making an acting career on stage? To find answers to the two questions we decided to sample opinion from those who are likely to ask the questions. We sampled opinions of students and staff in some of our post-primary institutions. Most of those whose opinions were sought had never had any formal lessons in drama although they know that plays are literary stories or accounts which are intended for performances on stage. They have all however had some opportunity of acting in plays of some sort or of watching performed plays.

We now present summaries of some of the answers received from school children between the ages of thirteen and twenty to the question: "Why should we study drama?"[2]

1. Drama aids in mental development.
2. It is recreative and entertaining.
3. It gives a sense of value and belonging to members of a play production group or organisation. In addition play acting promotes cordial relationship among members of a production.
4. It subdues shyness.
5. It offers a wide scope for discovering talent and for career opportunities.
6. It is an effective audio-visual teaching method - a practical and retentive approach to the study of other subjects.
7. As an aid to personality development and projection, it popularizes individual actors and actresses as well as their institutions.
8. Through the messages in the plays drama helps in moulding and producing socially fit and responsible citizens.
9. It exposes cultures for the appreciation of other people.
10. It improves one's expressiveness in a language.

---

[2] The survey of dramatic activities in past primary institutions was carried out between April and June 1975 in schools in Imo and Anambra States with funds made available through the Institute of African Studies, University of Nigeria, Nsukka.

11. Weekend rehearsals of plays are a form of continuing education which could be more rewarding than weekend travels

12. It stimulates a spirit of adventure in students.

13. It gives an insight into the real meaning of life and the practice of living.

14. It provides extra income.

15. It exercises the intellect and trains the memory in retention.

16. It improves school cultural and social environment.

17. It produces good public speakers.

18. It exposes culture contrast and facilitates the understanding of the habits arid style of living of other cultures.

19. It improves children's minds, breaches sex consciousness by encouraging a healthy social forum for the mixing of youths of both sexes.

20. It offers opportunities for education through travels to perform plays or watch other people's performances.

21. It indirectly teaches leadership through humility and followership.

22. It helps in the general understanding of life and humanity.

23. It reduces criminal tendencies by occupying some otherwise idle minds.

24. It is inspiring for it makes it possible for the youth to draw inspiration from the events and characters in plays.

25. One student out of a total of 1,358 students who returned their questionnaires volunteered the information that "Drama does nothing to improve anything".

We posed a similar question to post-primary school teachers of varying educational backgrounds. About ninety percent of them had received no formal lessons, in drama. But about seventy percent were actively involved in running school play production societies with or without the recognition or assistance of the school authorities. In general, staff answers agreed very much with those of the students with the following additional views:

1. Drama encourages team spirit and social tolerance among students.
2. It builds healthy, confident personalities.
3. It encourages discipline.

The above answers (staff and students) have been reproduced almost exactly as they were given. No distinction was made between drama as literature and practical drama (play production). Such a distinction was not deemed necessary since one is the extension of the other.

Let us now consider some other aspects of the question: "Why should we study drama?" "Why should drama not just be performed as an extra curricular activity involving only those who feel like it"?

Drama, like painting, sculpting, architecture, music and dance flourished as practical artistic disciplines practised by naturally gifted practitioners long before man started taking academic interest in them through the study of their forms, styles, values and typology. These critical attentions to their nature and structures influenced the formalization of standards and techniques, and helped to discipline their respective development. As time went on, not only did drama acquire a written form in addition to its extemporised and improvised form, but also literatures began to appear on how to prepare and apply the raw materials of drama for improved results; as well as on how to critically determine their values and qualities. As a result we now find it possible to start from the study of the discipline of drama as general education and move on to a specialisation in the field and in aspects of drama production (depending on one's aptitude or natural talents) whether as a profession or as a hobby.

Drama as a practical discipline like painting, sculpting, music, architecture, dance, etc still retains its primary attraction in the exhibited form; that is, the practical presentation of the finished product for visual appreciation by an aware audience.

The public exhibition is what gives the greatest meaning and credit to the ingenuity of the creators and executors (performers and artisans). The work of the architect finds fulfilment in the erected structure, that of the painter or sculptor as aesthetic or monumental exhibits in art galleries and other public as well as private places. The accomplishments of the musicians, the ingenuity of the dramatists and the expertise of the dancers find fulfilment when their creations are made to come alive on stage or screen (television or cinema) as audio-visual production of organised sounds, stories re-enacted by live actors, and demonstrated spatial rhythms of the human body respectively. Drama, however, has an additional advantage over other creative and performing arts disciplines: like the novel or poetry it finds further fulfilment as a literary art form.

The study of drama embraces its study through practical activity and its study as literature. But since the ultimate goal of writing of plays and the study of drama is the practical interpretation of the written form on stage as live-theatre, we are laying primary emphasis on the practice of drama. A branch of the living theatre, the practice of drama offers various areas of specialisation to talented people in disciplines other than acting. Such other fields of learning involved in drama in which people can specialise include music, plastic and costume arts, dance, business management, sound technology, lighting technology, public relations, etc.

Play production generally can be likened to the process of erecting a prefabricated building from conception to the appreciation of the finished building. For a building to be constructed somebody or an institution conceives the need for, and the idea of, the building. The conceiver approaches an architect, and passes on to him his vision of the building with specifications as to usage, size, etc. The architect then sets to work bearing in mind the given specifications. He reduces mere ideas into concrete impressions in the form of a preliminary sketch from which he designs the plan. From the plan he develops a working sketch and then, perhaps, a model.

Having finished constructing the building on paper (and often as a model) his sketches are passed on to a building contractor who is a specialist in organising and executing the construction of building plans. Quite often the contractor is not a building engineer but only an organiser. In such a case he should hire a civil building/engineer if he has none in his employ.

The civil/building engineer who interprets the architect's plan does not function alone. He works with a team of trained artisans who function under his direction. These include the foreman, the plumber, the electrician, the painter, the mason, the carpenter, the interior decorator, the public relations man or promoter, etc. Each and everyone of these artisans must possess specialised training or talent and be able to head a crew of journeymen in his own field. The building engineer who needs a working knowledge of all these areas of building technology has full responsibility for the structural erection of the building. His reputation is involved. He directs as well as supervises the work of every section. Should any of the sections fail to fulfil its task as specified, such inefficiency or inability will undermine the project and detract from the efforts of the other sections. It may even jeopardize the acceptability of the finished product.

If we compare the above process to play production - the staging of a work of drama (a play) - we discover that at times the conception of a play comes from outside the playwright. In such an instance he is commissioned by a body or an institution or an individual to write a play for a specific purpose. At other times the playwright, being a creative artist, conceives his own ideas and purposes for plays. Whichever way the theme comes to him, he, like the architect, sets to work to plan, plot, sketch and create out of the idea a composite finished structure in black and white called a play.

The play is now in need of a contractor who in the theatre is called a producer. The producer takes up the contract to convert the written form into a living edifice on stage for popular appreciation. Also like the building contractor he, the producer, could be an organiser or a financier without necessarily being a play director (executor). Where he is not the same person, the producer hands over the practical interpretation of the written play to this professional specialist - the director whose counterpart in the building industry is the civil/building engineer. Like the engineer, the play director is at the head of a team of specialist artisans, the foremost among whom is his foreman who in theatre is known as the Stage manager. Then there are the director's co-professtionals/specialists - the designers (scenic, lighting, costume) - each of whom works with a team of technicians and journeymen. Each of the designers could be a consultant to a particular production or a full time employee of an established theatre industry. The director also needs a promoter or business manager.

In drama the finished product is seen as the actors perform the written and executed work within specially designed and illuminated area - the stage. For every performance the actors, as well as the stage sets, lightning, props and other stage structures and properties, are assembled and set up as a composite exhibition in a rehearsed (pre-fabricated) order. So it is with the setting up of a prefabricated building in any given location. There could be a catastrophe should any of the artisans in a building site fall to accomplish his stipulated task well. It could equally be disastrous or at least inconvenient if not embarrassing should any artist, actor or any aspect of the pre-fabricated stage design fail to function as required and/or rehearsed. The entire enterprise would become an unsuccessful undertaking.

We should therefore study drama in schools because apart from giving scope for discovering and producing talented artists (actors, dancers and musicians), drama provides a practical workshop in inter-disciplinary cooperation. Play production calls for a division of the labour at the initial stages of a production. At the same time, team spirit and cooperation must pervade all the rehearsals and other activities before a play becomes a successful, finished and creditable product. In a school situation where facilities for practical theatre cannot be said to be ready-made, play production offers extra challenges to students and staff whose talents or inclinations may seem to be unrelated to drama.

For instance: scientifically inclined students in physics and chemistry could assist with the light and sound requirements for a play. Students with a flair for the liberal arts could handle publicity and programme. Students with an instinct for accounts and commerce could take charge of the business aspect of the production (procurements. gate fees, production-accounting, etc.) Students in secretarial studies could handle production of scripts, programmes, tickets and other secretarial jobs pertaining to the production. Students who have technological skills could tackle set-building and stage management. Budding plastic and decorative arts students as well as students skilled in engineering drawing would apply their ingenuity to the production of the various stage designs, costumes, painting and make-up. Musically talented students should help with any music required for the play; while those who are creative dancers could assist where the playwright or director requires stylized movement and dancing. Others in addition to those mentioned above who have keenness or talent to act would be given acting roles in the play. Staff members who are enthusiastic would find identity with the production by supervising or advising each section as their various talents, interests or specialisations apply.

With all hands on deck, cooperating and coordinated, a school play production exercise could become a miniature commonwealth of aspiring professionals. Students whose aspirations tend to be divergent would find a play production class a common platform that would excite their various aptitudes. A play production class, is therefore, a workshop, a meeting point for other school subjects - the sciences, the arts, commerce and handicraft. It offers opportunity for research, improvisation, experimentation, creativity and originality to every student.

In play production all activities need to be coordinated towards the needs of the play. There would be chaos if the various sections are given free rein to operate independently of the others. Such a coordinator we already know as a director. Apart from directing the actors on how he wants to interpret a play, the director of a play presides over a production committee comprising leaders of all the design, technical and promotion teams of a drama class.

From the above we can see that a drama class could constitute itself into a production class. And within the production class, students can belong to various production teams according to each student's potentialities. Where a student is not assigned an acting role in any particular production he would still find some stimulating fulfilment and a sense of belonging in the production. This is why when we talk of play production we do not imply only the director and his actors, but also every team member whether or not he/she is exhibited to the audience. At amateur and school levels those who are put on stage as actors should also be involved actively in one of the technical and artistic assignments. As a matter of principle every member of a drama class should know something of the functioning of the various production departments. It would be useful to rotate students from one section to the other. The experiences would be invaluable on and off stage.

Areas of Specialisation

Drama like most other disciplines of academic and technological pursuits, offers a wide range of opportunities for career specialisation. Some of these require that the student should be imaginative and creative while others merely require the acquisition of skill through training and practice. These career opportunities include: (a) directing, (b) acting, (c) script writing, (d) designing (light, costume, scenic) (e) choreography (t) make-up. These are the ones that require some basic creative talent on the part of the intending careerist. On the technological aspect of drama a student could specialize in Theatre Technology generally or in Theatre Management. There are other job opportunities in the theatre for technicians and artisans as stage carpenters, electricians, painters, seamstresses and stage hands. Even this class of theatre employees must learn the specialised aspect of their handicrafts although this could be acquired on the job once there is the basic knowledge.

Specialisation in any aspect of theatre industry would start after the aspirant has gone through a formal basic education which would qualify him/her for admission to institutions of higher learning that offer courses m aspects of theatre, or a conservatory where professionals are trained. Quite often though, some highly gifted actors do make it on stage without necessarily taking advanced courses in drama. Whether or not one undertakes further specialised studies, every aspect of theatre is primarily a practical profession and a period of diligent apprenticeship is necessary to grasp its technicalities and skill.

Careers in theatre are very rewarding. Although it is a new profession in our part of the world it is a primary industry in some other parts of the world. And in such places where theatre careers have flourished, we can say that many aspire towards careers on stage, but few are chosen because competition is quite high and only the hard-working best will survive. And those who break through and struggle to stay on top have lived to become celebrities and legends attracting more honours, awards and distinctions than are possible in any other profession. And that, in addition to their belonging to the topmost income bracket in such societies.

The Structure of a Play

We have already distinguished drama as being a literary art form. As such it has specialized literary distinctions which should be studied by every student as part of his/her essential basic liberal arts education. Drama as literature is more demanding in composition than its sister type - the novel.

A play is usually moulded into a structured form, although some playwrights especially modern writers could deliberately disorganise the form in their pursuit of artistic experimentation. The structural form of every good conventional play is made up of an introduction, a development, a climax, and a resolution. The playwright does not necessarily break up a play into chapters or movements on the basis of these distinctions. Rather he uses acts and scenes to divide the story into sections and subsections. A play is essentially a dramatized story. It is in the process of moving from scene to scene, and from act to act that the story teller takes us through the overall form from the introduction to the resolution of the story.

The introduction is the statement of the theme of the story. A play is written to be acted on stage for the benefit of an audience most of whom have not read the play. A playwright who fails to sustain the interest of his audience right from the beginning (introduction) of a play, through to the end (resolution) has failed to satisfy his audience, and has failed as a playwright. The first trick in playwriting is to get the story line across as tidily and vividly as possible without undermining the intelligence of the audience. There are, however, other factors that help to make a story-line worth the attention and investment of the audience. These will be discussed later. The introduction of a play which is the event with which the play opens is what is used to capture the interest of the audience. It caries the statement of the theme in which the protagonists are introduced. In it too, the style and the mood of a play are hinted even if not established; the location is determined and the tempo is set.

It would be a pity to start a story well and then lose grip, that is tempo and sense of direction, as it develops. The playwright, having captured the interest of his audience, must sustain it by feeding it with surprise after surprise i.e., structurally exposing and fitting in the pieces that will solve the puzzle (which is the crux of a play) by the final curtainfall. Every new structure added should make the audience eager for the next development. The next movement must not be too obvious. Every new bit must be a logical sequence to what happened before. So from the introduction the playwright makes use of elements of surprise and puzzle to create suspense and enhance interest. This period of guessing game (for the audience) is the development section of the play. It is the section that deals with counter-plots, sub-plots, intrigues and character establishment and consolidation. The playwright has to pace this section ingeniously so that there will be a consistent logical build-up of emotion and tension. For, should he lose his grip on the subject matter, or reveal his intentions by inadvertently announcing the fulfilment prematurely, the story ends at that stage, and whatever follows will be a boring anti-climax. As in a football match, when the result of the match is pre-empted by one side securing a wide goal lead, as well as an overwhelming superiority over their opponents, the spectators immediately lose interest. If they stay on to the end, it is just to while away time on an unexciting spectacle in which they have invested money and programmed their time. The playwright however is the seer who knows the result of his plotting. But to keep his audience on their feet, he continues balancing and counter-balancing the game, awarding and withdrawing advantages to various protagonists up till the climax which is the moment or section of catastrophe.

The climax section of a play is the highest peak in the build-up of tension and emotion; the period of utmost suspense when the audience holds its breath, afraid that to breath-down might fulminate disaster, the end of things. The climax section is like a precipice and requires great skill to handle especially if it has to last longer than a few minutes. Some playwrights like to end a play on the climax for special reasons or effects. This is not always satisfactory or successful. It does not offer emotional balance to the audience. There is usually a psychological necessity for an emotional exhaust, a catharsis, after a period of tension. Otherwise it is like a struggle that culminates in falling off a precipice and being left suspended in mid air. The usual technique in playwrighting is to provide an unforeseen tableau that offers a landing slope, a sort of life line, that will break, temper or extricate the catastrophe. Thereafter the play, like a journey, will strive for a conclusion, no matter the nature of the conclusion. Even in a tragedy the catastrophe is not necessarily the death of the principal subjects. That would be the inevitable catharsis. The catastrophe, i.e., the climax, is the inextricable nationalisation, the momentous causality that precipitates and necessitates the demise of the principal subject.

The conclusion is the resolution - resolution of the entanglements of the plot; resolution of emotions, of tensions, of suspense, of conflicts. After the climax the resolution must not be allowed to drag otherwise it could water down the suspense to a level that leaves the audience cold. That is if they have the courtesy to sit out such an infliction on their patience. A resolution is not an apologia. It is an inevitable summary proferred by the playwright for the events in the play. A poorly handled conclusion could prompt an audience walk-out, neutralise whatever was impressive in the main body of the play, in fact it could be the failure of the entire play. The recoup after the precipice - the catastrophe - should therefore be brisk and relevant in order to be effective.

So we can now see a play as a mountain climbing project involving ideationally and temperamentally diverse and unpredictable sojourners. The project starts with an assemblage of characters and their energetic brilliant take-off through the forest, everybody and every track pointing resolutely towards the peak - this is the introduction.

As they embark on, and tackle, the tense, unpredictable ascent with their various aims, techniques and inter-relations - that is the development.

The suspension (between earth and heaven) occasioned by the unknown forces attendant at the peak of the mountain, or merely the conquest of the top, constitutes the climax.

The fast descent or salvation from the peak to find identity with the earth, the starting point, and the familiar forces is the conclusion.

Style and Technique of Composition

A good theme, a good story line, a succession of progressive tightly bound sequences, these alone do not make the written play. Other factors are usually taken into account in the realisation of a play as a literary art form. One of these factors is the technique of presentation. The dialogue technique is the most common technique. In the written form; stage directions are used as guides in creating the locations, the characters, the movements and the moods. But these could also be woven into the dialogue proper. In the exhibited form of a play the actors and artists interpret the stage directions, whether inserted separately in the script or implied in the dialogue, for the benefit of the audience. The style of scripting - the technique of unveiling the story and action through the dialogues and indicated stage movements, also the arrangement of the sequences of the story into acts and scenes, vary from one playwright to another as well as from one type of play (given the same author) to the other. All these constitute the study of drama as a literary art form and this study determines the successful interpretation of a play as a live-art form.

Characterisation is also an essential feature of drama both as a literary form and as an exhibited art form. The novel has scope for detailed description of characters. In a play, characterisation is a more difficult task. Temperament, style of expression, physique, age, sex and mannerism of each and every character must be well defined and distinguished from those of the others through dialogue and prescriptive stage direction. It is the characters in a play that determine the nature and scope of development of a given theme or plot. As a matter of fact the themes for plays are limited but the variation of plots are made limitless by the pecularities of the characters and character types featured in each treatment of a given theme or plot. On stage the issue of characterisation is solved for the audience by the distinctions between the various actors with respect to voice, physique, age, sex, mannerisms, costume, sets, props, etc. The study of drama as a literary form involves the study of characterisation as implied in the dialogue of any given play. The detailed study of characterisation in a given play is prerequisite for the choice of actors (casting) by the director, and the effective interpretation of such characters on stage by those who will act in the play.

Treatment of location is another important aspect of drama as written art form. It may not always be possible, for instance, to create certain events, scenes or situations physically on stage. A novel has no such problems. Detailed descriptions of places, moods and events as in the novel are not always effective techniques in a play. In plays, a journey through rapids or a forest, although a favourite technique in films, cannot be realised live on stage except as narrative. There is therefore a limit imposed by practicability in locating scenes and actions in a play. Although technology has helped out with creating or simulating representative, often facsimile, locations (sets and scenic designs), moods (colours and lighting), and even illusions of personalities, events or situations (make up, mechanical and sound effects) in the performed version of plays, the literary form requires great ingenuity to portray locations and moods vividly. The playwright has to build all these into the dialogue. The stage directions must be sketchy, otherwise he will be writing a novel. Literary study of drama, therefore, also involves a study of locations, moods, events and situations as implied or stated in the dialogue, as well as the playwright's technique of establishing them.

As can be seen from the above, drama is a unique literary art form. Its study is important not only as a study of its specialised creative skill in language, structure and form but also as a pre-requisite for a meaningful interpretation of a play as a performed art.

The study of drama as literary art form is also the study of the personality of playwrights, their society, their environment and other factors that influence their creativity and style. It is equally a study of the factors that determine dramatic activity. The foremost of these factors is the venue for play performances.

If there is no venue there cannot be dramatic activity and the impetus to write at all would be greatly diminished. The playwright's greatest ambition is to see his play performed. An unperformed play is an archival document not a play. Venue determines the scope and intensity of dramatic activity in any society. A playwright bears in mind the nature of his possible performance venue (amphitheatre, open air theatre, i.e. theatre in the round, proscenium theatre, revolving theatre, platform theatre, etc.) when determining the size of his cast, the locations of his scenes, and the activities that he can incorporate.

Another major factor that determines dramatic activity is the society. Apart from its function as an entertainment and educational medium, drama can also be a powerful vehicle for social and political commentary. Dramatic activity can therefore be determined by the nature of freedom and encouragement it enjoys within a given social and political set-up. And since drama has to be performed, and for an intelligent and critical live audience, the social and political attitudes of an audience in a given environment go a long way to determine the nature and constancy of drama presentation in that environment. The social attitudes will, for instance, influence participation in dramatic activity, the thematic thrust of plays performed, as well as the overall development of theatre as a viable and utilitarian venture.

Chapter 3

Types Of Plays

Although drama is conceptually a practical art form, the execution of its practical projection will be handicapped if the performers and technicians fail to grasp the fundamental nature of their most important raw material - the play script. In the preceding chapter we discussed some of the factors that determine the literary form and the mechanics of drama. The particular way in which such factors affect a play is in turn determined by the typology of plays. In this chapter therefore we are going to distinguish the various types of plays, noting as we do so, that the typology of a play determines the dialogue style, the acting style, the actor-personality, the technical support for the artists, and the ideal audience reaction.

There are two primary types of plays: the tragedy and the comedy. There are secondary types of plays which are derivations of the two primary types and which are distinguished by the variations in the treatment given by the playwright. The major secondary types of plays are the melodrama and farce. Other lesser types are tragicomedies, festival plays, chronicle plays, dance drama, heroic plays and burlesques.

It is not really possible to give an absolute definition of any of the types of plays. It is not possible either to give rigid specifications as to the structural form of each. This is primarily so because a play is first and foremost the off-spring of a uniquely creative personality. It acquires the expressive personality of the particular human creator who as a skilled artisan (not necessarily formally trained in the art) formulates this offspring (theme and plot) into a composite art form. In arriving at the final product he may or may not conform to conventional models and methodology. Nevertheless the nature of his plot and his approach to its development discipline his work into a classifiable typology. There is also the important effect environmental circumstances prevailing at any given time have on the playwright. These circumstances influence the creative process of a play and thus the final outcome of the playwright's typological visions. There are standard qualitative factors, however, which are used in classifying plays into types. The major factors include: (a) treatment of characters, (b) nature and treatment of plot, (c) the general mood of the play (light or serious), (d) the thematic source. These factors have been arrived at, not necessarily from the evaluation of plays by critics, but, primarily according to the general impressions and emotions each type of play generates in an aware and ideal audience. In other words the typical emotive responses of theatre audiences have helped to categorize play types. In some contemporary societies all over the world, theatre critics have undertaken analytical determination of play types on behalf of and in the interest of their theatre audiences with varying degrees of acceptability. In spite of the critics, who quite often cannot hide their personal prejudices, the ideal audience always retains the ultimate verdict on the type and success of a play.

In attempting to define and describe types of plays, we should also bear in mind that there have been variations in determining what qualities should qualify a typology from one period of theatre history to another. However, certain qualities of each type have to run consistently through all the periods of drama history to guide us in classifying plays of all times. These lake into consideration the divergencies within each type occasioned by the social and artistic peculiarities of the various periods. Thus we talk, for instance, of Greek tragedy/comedy; Medieval tragedy/comedy and Modern tragedy/comedy. And we are now at the stage of including Modern African tragedy/comedy.

Tragedy

Perhaps the first documented attempt to define tragedy as a literary typology was by the great 4th Century B.C.

philosopher, Aristotle. He defined tragedy as "an imitation of an action that is serious, complete and of a certain magnitude..." which employs the elements of pity and fear or terror to effect a purgation of such emotions in the audience. He based his definition on a study of the plays before and during his time, as well as on the emotional appreciation of the plays by their audiences. Starting from Aristotle's evaluation at his time, through tragedy of all ages, and arriving at our present times, we continue to see and evaluate tragedy as a serious treatment of a theme that is weighty, involving plots and characters of impressive depth and magnitude.

Tragedy does not necessarily involve the death of a principal character. Tragedy is essentially a disastrous event. The disaster can emanate from an ideology, a philosophy, a belief, a way of life or from a particular society, institution, or person. As a dramatic type, tragedy typifies man's eternal struggle against fate or other such unalterable situations in life. The struggle usually ends in futility, although playwrights at times make allowances for a form of redemption for the favourable party in order to balance the intense emotions excited.

Religion formed the basis of early tragedy, the Greek tragedy — as is extant in the works of Aesychlus 525-456 B.C., Sophocles, 497-405 B.C. and Euripedes 485-400 B.C. The Greek religion revolved around a hierarchy of gods who wielded great influences, or participated actively in the lives of their people, advancing the aspirations and causes of the humans they favoured; while thwarting the fortunes of those whom they disliked, or those who found favour with rival gods. Quite often these gods visited the earth in human form to discharge their missions. At other times they invoked the elements or animal forms and symbols, and used them to accomplish or establish their intentions. They also had certain obligations assigned to them by their people as a group. These obligations were often expected to be fulfilled in manifestable forms. Greek tragedies (usually referred to as classical, i.e., ideal tragedy), became successful masterpieces because the people of the time were strongly bound to their system of beliefs. In a society where there is no effective system of beliefs, it would be difficult to produce a tragedy that would go down emotively with the audience. Such is the tendency with 20th-century tragedy in a world that has no effective universality of beliefs even within a given homogeneous society.

Like Greek tragedy, the dominant effective themes for successful African tragedy are the traditional religions, beliefs, customs, ethics, and precepts. The conflicting, often disastrous, impact of Western civilisation and its attendant revolutionization of our traditional ways of life have produced human and socio-political upheavals, often of most disturbing consequences. These conflicts also constitute powerful themes for unique African tragedy under the pen of enterprising playwrights.

Another quality of a tragedy is its universality of appeal. A true tragedy always has relevance to the life experiences (current or historical) of all peoples. The situation may be foreign to the audience but the emotional stresses of any true tragedy must find some identity with any theatre audience in any given human society.

The acting area, occasions for presentations, as well as audience characteristics have greatly influenced dramatic form and the setting of plays in various ways at various periods of drama history. Greek plays were performed in an open air stadium in the form of an amphitheatre comprising large semi-circular rows of seats fashioned out of a hillside. This audience are - auditorium - enclosed a circular dancing area called the orchestra. The orchestra had a small stone altar of Dionysus called thymele (a structural reminder of the religious origin of the plays. Greek plays started as religious tributes to Dionysus, Bacchus, the god of wine and fun). Facing the auditorium on the other side of the orchestra was the stage. Behind the stage a scene building formed the dressing rooms as well as background for action. Greek tragedy made extensive use of a chorus located in the orchestra. In addition to executing a range of songs and dances, the function of the chorus was to explain actions, scenes and events not represented on stage. They also set and interpreted the moods and conflicts of the actors. In short they ran commentaries on the issues of the play. The Greek chorus remained on stage throughout a play.

Actors in Greek tragedy were limited in number to about two or three. They earned the title "actors" because they had all the speaking parts that constituted dialogue. There could be "extras": characters who had less important roles to portray. It is interesting to note that women were never allowed to appear on Greek stage or on Roman stage which followed it. Masks were freely used by actors to represent various characters as well as impersonate female characters.

Occasions for performing Greek tragedy were during religious festivals associated with the worship of Dionysus.

Extant examples of Greek tragedy include: Aeschylus: *Againennon, The Libation Bearers'* etc. Sophocles: *Oedipus Rex, Anti gone* etc; Euripides: *Hippolytus, Electra. Medea, The Madness of Heracles,* etc.

Another golden period for tragedy was the Elizabethan period in England - the period between 1584 and 1642 AD. This was the time of one of the foremost names of all times in drama - Shakespeare. The Elizabethan theatre was partly covered and partly open air. The uncovered part was the centre -the pit - of the theatre where those who paid the lowest gate fee of about one penny were allowed to stand. The theatre was octagonal in shape with rows of galleries and seats for those who paid higher gate fees. There were three parts to the Elizabethan stage: First was a more or less rectangular platform jutting into the pit with the "a-penny-each" crowd standing at its sides. The bulk of stage activity took place on this platform. Behind the platform and forming the eighth side of the octagonal theatre on the lowest gallery was the inner stage. The inner stage had a curtain which cut it off when no action was located there. It was used for small scenes like bedroom scenes. The third part of the Elizabethan stage was the upper stage immediately above the inner stage, and on the same level as the second gallery of the theatre.

Both this upper stage and the platform had low railings. The upper stage in addition had a curtain for screening it when acting was not taking place there. It was the ideal location for scenes set in high places - say on top of a tree, a balcony, a mountain, etc.

Although women were still not allowed on stage, Elizabethan plays required a large team of speaking characters of both sexes and very little, though effective, use of the chorus, Greater emphasis was laid on character development and portrayal. There was great emphasis also on dramatic action although scenic representation was not thought to be very important. The themes of Elizabethan tragedy were dominantly social and political.

Elizabethan audiences demanded lots of action to pep up dialogues and oratories in plays. The audience was comprised of all classes of the society located at demarcated areas of the theatre. Those closest to the actors were those who could be expected to exhibit rude manners in expressing their reactions to a performance. They were also the class that would be thrilled more by action than by monotonous refinement of language. But all classes of the audience were interested in a good story: an absorbing story line, romance of language, romance of stage action.

Shakespeare was the most outstanding writer of this period. To his credit are such ever popular tragedies as: *Hamlet, Romeo and Juliet, Anthony and Cleopatra, Macbeth* etc.

Tragedy in the modern period of drama history has not been as important as in the preceding periods. African drama, however, offers great potential for true tragedies in the classical and contemporary idioms. African traditional drama is involved or implied in our numerous festivals in which dances, music and rituals feature rather prominently. Exhibited dramatic action has centred around a few actors. An entire performance can be a sequence of pageants programmed over a number of days. Some call for change of venues. African traditional drama has been integrated so much with other aspects of theatre and life that some of the essential elements of (literary) drama tend to be subsumed and obscured by the emphasis on pageantry and ceremonials generally referred to as celebrations. The open air and campfire theatre-in-the-round are typical of African theatre types. African traditional theatre can boast of empathic participant audiences. The dramatic truth might not be obvious in the enaction but it has always been intrinsic in the festival theme and the preferred symbols. The ritual aspects of the festivals have been marked by strong psychological as well as dramatic suspense; while the catharsis of the festival theme/story (whether taken for granted or acted out) has been manifested in the form, elaborateness and emphasis given to music-making, dances and feasting featured in the festival. These have been presented as dramatic anecdotes, deriving from the theme, and encourage participant-audiences.

Contemporary African playwrights are now investigating the submerged, implied and expressed dramatic contents of African traditional festival themes. Such are those stories that have been taken for granted by a society in its festival presentation possibly because they were presumed as common knowledge to members of the society; but which are not explained to outsiders in the emphasized elements of the festival enaction.

African literary drama, which is a contemporary development, identifies with the established scope and structure of drama through the ages. It has the advantage of the historical trends in written drama. The unique features of new African drama, therefore, are not found in the language, literary style or form; not in the venue for presentation and its type of stage; not even in the peculiarities of its audience, rather in the socio-political implications of the themes from which most of them spring as well as in the style of presentation.

There tends to be greater scope for tragedies than comedies in the themes of African traditional drama which are derived from the traditional religious and belief systems as well as from the conflicts of socio-cultural evolutions and revolutions. Even in literary thematic resources, the social, political and economic imbroglio in the African milieu leaves the people in sour mood to appreciate comedies.

The trends in African tragic drama can be seen in the works of De Graft: *Through a Film Darkly;* Efua Sutherland: *Edufa:* Zulu Sofola: *Wedlock of the Gods,* Ola Rotimi: *Kurunmi;* Tregaye Gabre-Medhim: *Oda Oak Oracle;* Lewis Nkosi: *The Rhythm of Violence,* among others.

Comedy

Although comedy is a primary drama type it is difficult to give a definition which could embrace all varieties within it while excluding other drama types. An attempt at a working definition of a comedy would be: a lighthearted but noble treatment of a piquant theme. The inadequacy of this definition is immediately apparent in any attempt to define what constitutes a noble treatment or a piquant theme. Suffice it however to say that an audience should be able to leave a comedy performance with a cheered spirit, some mental stimulation as well as some message through all the fun.

The qualities of a comedy have varied through drama history. But all through the periods the elements of hilarity, satire, romance (of language and theme), ridicule, and follies have characterised comedy.

The Greeks had their religious and social comedies, and Aristophanes was an outstanding writer. As was the case with the origin of tragedy, comedy was started in honour of Dionysus, and dwelt on the revelry concept of Dionysus as Bacchus, the god of wine. Greek comedies also sprang from fertility festivals in honour of the same god.

The performance features of Greek tragedy were also found in the comedy: a chorus of 24 whose costumes and performances, however, included high spirited songs, dances and general revelry: two or three actors were also involved as protagonists. Plot was not emphasized in the comedies. Greek comedy could therefore be described as hilarious and satirical entertainment with pungent though oblique comment on the society. In Aristophanes' *Lysistrata,* male sex symbols were worn on stage to emphasize the emotional ravages and deprivations of the theme which satirized war. Some of Aristophanes' other titles are also suggestive: *The Birds. The Frogs* and *The Knights.*

By the Elizabethan period, romantic and realistic comedy with easy to follow story-lines were developed. Music, song and dance continued to be features of comedy. They helped to enhance its light-hearted mood. Shakespeare's romantic comedies: *Twelfth Night* and *As YOU Like It* are popular examples. The eighteenth century audience loved comedies of virtue, morality and manners. Modem comic writers have produced prototypes of comedies that have been loved all through the ages.

Melodrama and Farce

Melodrama is a freer form of tragedy while farce is a loose form of comedy. Quite often the differences are not easily discerned and we are tempted at times to classify all plays as either tragedy or comedy. The fundamental difference between the primary types or their secondary derivations is seen not necessarily in the subject matter (tragedy and melodrama share the same serious subject matters, while comedy and farce share the same lighter treatment of the stimulating issues of life). The difference is seen in the handling of the story.

The origin of the word melodrama was in association with serious plays that had musical accompaniments, hence melo(s)-drama. Melodrama could easily be illustrated with the musically orchestrated *Ira gedie specie* characterised by happy endings which we watch on the cinema and television screens. The early nineteenth century featured tragedies with essential musical accompaniment. Although music was eventually dropped except as incidental in a play, the term melodrama was retained as descriptive of the mood treatment of serious themes.

Whereas tragedy emphasizes characters and therefore the plot is dominated by the quality of the characters, melodrama, which emphasizes thrills, lays more emphasis on plot and sensational situations than on character development. Characters in melodrama generally conform to known types — prototype characters. The writer thus gains freedom from character development to dwell on thrilling episodic treatment of the subject matter. In its pursuit of thrills, melodrama makes its characters accomplish ordinarily unlikely feats for the sole purpose of providing sensational moments for the excitation of the audience.

Farce gives ridiculous treatment to the subject matter of comedy in order to solicit mere laughter. In farce as in melodrama the plot dominates, manipulates and ridicules the characters. This tends to unduly exaggerate events in the story. Farce also tends more than comedy to emphasize physical action, leaving little room for intellectual treatment of the subject matter. Generally, however, the distinction between farce and comedy is not as pronounced as that between melodrama and tragedy. Unlike the latter two types, farce and comedy share a common audience appeal — lighthearted and spirited entertainment, The degree of simplicity in the treatment of character as well as the subject matter with which they solicit for such appeal varies. Comedy offers recognizable intellectual quality in the treatment of subject matter, and greater nobility in the presentation of its characters.

Our Audience's Tastes

Applying the above distinction of drama types to our African audiences, it has been observed that melodrama and farce (which are closer in mood to our high-spirited traditional theatre types), succeed more at all levels than tragedy and high comedy. This explains why the very farcical and melodramatic folk operas of Hubert Ogunde, Duro Ladipo, Ogunmola and others attract larger enthusiastic audiences than the intellectual plays of Wole Soyinka or J.P. Clark. The generality of our audiences go all out for thrills, sensations, laughter and unrestrained excitement, and tend to have little interest in works of intellectual depth. We have an audience that goes to a theatre primarily to be thrilled and amused on the spot, and not necessarily to be intellectually stimulated. A contemplative audience appreciates tragedies and high comedies, while an emotional audience cares primarily for farce and melodrama whether on the stage or on the screen. The contemporary African theatre audience is preponderantly an emotional audience. And this poses serious problems for serious-minded writers and producers in contemporary Africa whose works are patronised by only a negligible percentage of the population.

Our audience preferences, as have been indicated above, agree with our traditional theatre background. The melodrama and farce are very close to our traditional theatre forms because they exploit traditional dramatic (even if not our spiritual) theatre elements: thrills, sensations, laugh-provoking episodes and expletives, spirited music and dance, effective and often grotesque costumery, exaggerated character traits and copious burlesques. The employment of these elements of pure entertainment tend to obscure the importance of the subject matter, and equally drain the characters of such personal qualities that make a tragedy a drama of intense subject matter and distinguished characters. Because of this traditional background, our contemporary theatre audience does not so much care for a tight plot or a distinct story-line in a play presentation as it does for thrilling episodes that may constitute an incoherent plot or obscured subject matter. For the same reasons our audience does not seem particular about realistic situations so long as they are getting their money's worth of sheer entertainment.

As a result of our traditional heritage, musical drama (plays that involve integrated, instead of incidental, music or music and dance activities), appeal immensely to our audiences at all levels whether the play is intrinsically a tragedy or melodrama, a comedy or farce. But the audience is equally particular about finding some identity with the music. That is to say, whether the music is the traditional type or a contemporary """" music species using Western instruments, it is welcome. On the other hand any music that has not been culturally accepted, like classical music or oriental music, would distract their interest in the play. Traditional music and dance which are irrelevant to a play but which are inserted (as most directors are now tempted to do) merely to solicit cultural acceptability do not go down well with most audiences. These attitudes point towards the fact that our audiences do not want a serious play told too seriously. We are passing through a period of "liquid" theatre, i.e. a synthesis of drama, music and dance.

Before stage plays started gaining any audiences outside scattered school attempts at Shakespeare and Sheridan, the cinema had already become a popular theatre medium in West Africa. The cinema drew its clientele from all works and classes of the society, and some theatre houses provided separate seating areas for these classes just as in the Elizabethan theatre. The ordinary people paid a few pennies and sat or stood on benches on the ground floor while those who could afford to pay a few shillings sat on better chairs on raised areas or on balconies. The appeal of the cinema, which is an urban entertainment medium, centres mainly on: (a) the hero image it offers, i.e., the star actors and actresses whose names have become more popular than even those of the leaders in government, (b) elements of mood music which pace the sensational episodes; or music and dance included as episodes of sheer spectacular interest, (c) extravagant and sensational episodes of pursuits, romance and fights, often meaningless and irrelevant to the story.

Our audiences look at the drama theatre as a poor substitute for the thrills of the cinema. Without bothering about the physical limitations posed by the stage on production as compared to the cinema, they expect stage drama to mount the full range of the cinematic wonders, scenery and splashes of panoramic sensations.

The hero-image appeal technique of the cinema will be an asset in the establishment of a viable drama movement in the near future. But we direly lack the stage actors who would offer such a booster. We also need hero-figures among our practising directors and playwrights. The few who have succeeded in establishing their images (even as hobby-practitioners), have proved to be amazing crowd pullers. This is a reassuring pointer to the fact that no matter what we say about our audiences, they are merely waiting for their stage personalities to project themselves and then sell their wares. An indicator of the great future which literary theatre could enjoy in Africa is that our audiences, even in our traditional societies, love and patronize theatre stars. This love for stars was transferred to foreign film stars on the introduction of public cinemas. Recent observations do show that the African audience appreciates African theatre stars more than foreign film stars on condition that such local stars continue to live up to artistic expectation. It then looks as if the greatest obstacle to the arrival of the golden age of African drama theatre is the non-emergence of professional star actors (since a working crop of playwrights and directors are already emerging).

Chapter 4

Stage-craft

Drama is not life but an imitation of life. The art of play-acting which is stage-craft is not necessarily taught as one would teach mathematics. It is a guided learning. Every actor would always bring into play his/her personality and originality (consciously or otherwise) in every guided situation. Also through personal training an actor could master his/her emotions and expressions sufficiently to interpret any given situation.

The aim of this chapter therefore is not necessarily to teach how to act. Rather we are going to call attention to those qualities which when consciously inculcated or subconsciously applied, are the characteristics of good acting. Conscious acquisition of acting techniques comes through self-discipline and practice while the subconscious demonstrations are a result of drawing out those inherent qualities that are natural or possible in the actor as a unique human personality.

Dimensions of Dramatic Activity

There are two dimensions of dramatic activity which every aspiring actor must be conscious of before considering going on stage. These are: (a) the dialogue - the spoken story of the play, and (b) the action - the mimed story of the play. This immediately suggests that we can act through the spoken word, i.e what we say and how we use our voices to say them; and through movement, portraying meaning in every activity or inactivity of any part of our body, be it the head, the face, the eyes, the nose, the shoulder, the hands, the fingers, the trunk, the hips, the legs, etc.

In radio plays only one dimension of dramatic activity is required, that is, the dialogue supplemented with sound effects. The forte of the film is on action. To appreciate this it is important to remind ourselves that the film industry started with silent films which depended solely on expressive acting - mime and movement - to tell the story. And one of the greatest all-time stars the film industry has produced who exemplified these characteristics, Charlie Chaplin, was a star of the silent film era. Up to the present time the film (with its advantages of close up on features, as well as unrestricted mobility of its camera eye), continues to rely more on the action effect than on the dialogue effect to portray its stories. How many of us are able to catch or understand half the words spoken in any films we've attended? Why are Indian films, Chinese films, French film and other films in languages unintelligible to us popularly appreciated in spite of the language barrier? Granted that some of these foreign language films carry subtitles (which apart from being distractions are inadequate summaries of the dialogue), we have depended largely on the second dimension of dramatic activity — *action* — to understand the story enacted in films. Sound effects supplement all theatre activities whether on radio, film or stage. Other effects —mechanical and light — which are not effective on radio go a long way to compliment and enhance film and stage activities.

If we have now understood that the forte for radio plays is in dialogue while that for the film is in action, what about stage plays? Stage plays lay equal emphasis on the two fortes (verbal and non-verbal) of communication in order to produce a successful performance. That is to say, good stage acting demands that the actor on stage balances the two dimensions of dramatic activity. That is why it is more difficult to be a good stage actor than to be either a radio or film actor. As a matter of fact, a good radio play actor who relies on voice acting does not automatically make a good stage actor. Similarly a good film actor, endowed with appropriate physical qualities, proficiency in mimes and physical expressions, would not necessarily make a good stage actor. A good stage actor combines the stated qualities of the radio play actor and the film actor to make a successful impression in the stage medium of acting.

Stage drama poses other extra challenges in preparation and production than the other media of theatre such as radio and television. A radio theatre actor is merely an audio-artiste. For that advantage he/she does not need to memorise his/her lines. Some rehearsals on voice production and emphasis on vocal acting are all that are required. The actor could, and usually does take his/her lines straight from the script, being careful not to rustle the sheets in front of the microphone. The film actor could take his/her dialogue in bits of scenes, and in any order preferred by the director and suggested by the locations for shooting. In some instances, for good film actors with poor memories, some aid devices are used to help them pick their lines while "on camera." But for the stage actor, the lines must be very well memorised from the beginning to the end before meaningful rehearsals can be held. Thereafter the stage actor still has a lot of things to worry about: his movements, his expressions (audio or visual), his positions which are blocked in advance, the unpredictable distractions of his/her co-artistes during performances, the possibility of an embarrassing slip or omission in the provision or arrangement of his/her props which must be covered up, audience distractions, technical failures, the uncomfortable knowledge that nothing portrayed (whether right or wrong) can be retrieved or edited over. These factors, moreover, must be considered in each presentation of a stage play.

In radio, production can be halted if there is the minutest hitch, and recording can start all over again. Or, a re-recording of the faulty section may be preferred. Or dubbing and excision from several recordings of the same play, called editing, could be made to produce the master copy. In the film, several "takes" of a scene, or a fragment of a scene, or a single movement, could be made so that the best "takes" could be edited and any mistakes discarded. But on stage there is only one opportunity to do everything correctly, especially when rehearsals have been concluded and the play is put on for an audience. Any major mistakes (of line or movement) during a public show could ruin hours, days and weeks of exerting industry, It is for these reasons that we insist that the stage actor must master his/her lines of the dialogue very confidently before rehearsals are scheduled to start. It is equally of immense advantage to the actor if he/she knows the lines of any other character acting against him/her. At the same time the actor must know the story very well indeed and understand his/her pseudo-personality, that is, the character he/she is portraying in the play, well enough before stepping on to the rehearsal stage. These done, the actor will then be better conditioned to worry about the other artistic, technical and human problems or distraction of the stage, as well as the director's wishes with respect to interpretations, during both rehearsals and performances.

Another area in which stage drama makes greater demands on the artistes than either radio drama or film is in the constancy of personal appearances. With radio and film the performance is recorded on tape or celluloid and repeated thereafter as many times as desired. Copies could even be made and dispatched to any places they are required so that the actors do not have to move in person for the purposes of showing their performances. Stage drama requires that the artistes should put up physical appearances every time and every place a performance of the finished play is scheduled, to say exactly the same line and to execute virtually the same movements. When we consider that in some societies in the world one single play could run for as many as 365 days and possibly for six out of even seven days of the week during the 365 days, we can appreciate the magnitude of work and discipline a stage artiste is subjected to by his/her profession. In order to take care of any unforeseen human disappointments through ill health and the like after the audience has booked and programmed attendances to a play that is running, theatre companies usually have understudies who can substitute in an emergency for an unavoidably absent actor. And many a stage star has been spotted and promoted as a result of their brilliant performances as substitutes for scheduled stars. Another precaution that ensures that a play which has a long run does not disappoint its audience as a result of human failings is to double cast the principal actors especially. This method also gives the principal artistes time off to relax while their doubles take their turns.

The Beginning Actor

Having discussed the two dimensions of dramatic activity as they affect the various drama media, and also why a stage actor has more to worry about than his/her radio or film counterpart, let us consider some qualities of a good stage actor.

A good stage actor matures from self-consciousness to conscious habits. By the time the techniques of stage acting become habit such an aspirant has arrived in the profession and could be called an actor. Self consciousness characterises the period of apprenticeship. Some actors are made through self-development. Others are natural actors in that acting becomes them naturally.

It is bad habit, and an indication of lack of self-confidence for an artiste to use debilitating aids (like drugs or drinks), which give false courage, to try and quell the invasion of nerves which naturally assails performers before and often while facing the lights on stage. Such extraneous aids for combating stage fright do get out of control quite often and ruin the show as well as the reputation, career and even the life of an artiste. Induced acting is a degradation of the prestige of the profession. The actor could easily become addicted as greater and greater doses are progressively needed to steady his weakened nerves until he becomes a mental and physiological decrepit, and thus a discredited and discarded actor. And many a promising as well as brilliant stage career has been ruined by this show of weak self-discipline.

Like a soldier into battle, a stage artiste must brave the challenges of this stage fright by mustering abundant self-will. Here are a few tips on how to combat stage fright - the monster which has scared many a talented artiste away from the stage.

First of all you must ensure that you have made adequate personal preparations for a performance:

(a) You must be so confident with your lines and movements that you can reproduce them automatically even when the lights dazzle and mesmerize you.

(b) You must be punctual to a performance. An actor who arrives for a performance at the moment he/she is just about to be "On" is usually rushed, confused and, therefore, nervous. Moreover such an actor invites chances of being further harassed by a worried director, stage manager, make-up artist and fellow actors thereby escalating his/her nervousness.

(c) You must further avoid anything that will agitate you before a show by ensuring that your costumes and properties are handy and in good shape long before the show starts. Cross check on the state and location of your costumes and props as soon as you arrive for every show. A missing property, or an unserviceable property, or a ruined costume discovered at the moment of going on stage could put you off guard, make you self-conscious and increase your stage fright. The stage manager, the property man and the wardrobe mistress should not be taken too much for granted. They are conscientious but fallible human beings. As a good and cooperative actor you must always cross check with those who handle your stage equipments if you do not want to gamble with your rating, career, and reputation. Remember that the audience does not know about any backstage hands. You are the one they see, know, appreciate or discredit as the case many be by what you do.

An artiste who expects to be pampered and worshipped by fellow team members is a nuisance, a disappointment to the profession and his/her colleagues. Such an actor will be the architect of his/her own disgrace and downfall. You must understand that nobody is more useful than the other person to a performance. For instance, if it is required that an actor playing a low-rated servant's role should hand over a whip on cue to the principal actor in a play, and the servant misses such a cue, the principal immediately looks a fool and is noticeably distracted, perturbed. The servant (who is a minor) is, therefore, as useful as the principal for the success of the principal's acting, as well as of the entire performance, although the principal technically has a major role to play.

Another technique for combating stage fright is a psychological one, especially after all the foregoing precautions have been taken. You must bear in mind that it takes a lot of guts to stand up to face and address an audience. This, anybody who has attempted public speaking should know. And going on stage for the first time is like having a nightmare. Stage fright is the monster that gives one the jitters during his/her first entries whenever the call for a performance is made. This monster (although it can be outgrown) can shadow an actor all through his/her career especially at the opening of every new show. So an actor, more especially a beginning actor must always make brother-courage a constant companion.

It takes more guts to address a critical audience than to address a mob or a political rally. The latter relies on mob courage (psychology), while the former calls for personal courage. Many people who are ordinarily bright and blustery become dull, weak-kneed wrecks when spot-lighted to face a critical audience. On the other hand, most stage charmers have a withdrawn, often low profile demeanour in ordinary social interactions.

The mere fact that an actor has pluck enough and quality enough to perform before an audience, the feeling of importance that the distinguished audience is there for the sole purpose of honouring him for his performance, should give the actor a feeling of superiority over the audience. If anybody in that audience has as much courage and expertise as the actor, that member of the audience should have been with him on stage. Once the actor understands and feels convinced that he is the best person to be doing what he is doing, which is why he is doing it as far as the performance goes, then he should aggrandize that superiority feeling, though without a swagger. Superiority complex engenders self-confidence with which to browbeat any audience. But the homework must be well done.

(e)   As a beginning actor, the performer should not attempt to locate faces in the audience; but to see it as indistinguishable mass of faces. In an attempt to catch a crony's encouraging wink, smile or sign, you may instead confront an austere face that could shatter your composure. The audience as a body will communicate the appropriate mode of encouragement for your acting if it is merited.

(f)   It is very vital for an actor to be composed before and during a performance. In fact, composure is the tonic for confident acting. To achieve that composure, one must make time to relax for about one hour, sleeping or just relaxing, immediately before a show. After relaxing and taking a bath, the actor should feel fresh and refreshed. Any tension or tenseness he may have been feeling would be relaxed. He should then arrive for the performance much composed and in good time, to avoid any irritations. An actor, amateur or professional, who cherishes his public image should not gamble with his contacts with that public, in this case the stage audience who could make or unmake not only his career but his sense of achievement which is required for a person to make a success of any career. It would be a terribly frustrating experience to be booed or ignored by an audience for performing poorly.

If after taking the above precautions, an actor still feels a tingling assault of nerves, then the emergency treatment is a brief breathing and movement exercise immediately before facing the lights. Breathe in fully and slowly, expanding the lungs. Then breathe out slowly, relaxing your entire body. A deep full breath in the lungs is a wonderful balm when the blood is racing unusually because of tenseness. When on stage, the actor should take a preparatory deep breath, deliberately, and with its support attack the first line. The chances are that all other things being taken care of, the nibbling nerves will be exhaled with that breath.

Types of Actors

A "regulation" actor is the actor who, through training, observation, and perseverance acquires the skill of character and situation portrayal which is called acting. A "natural" actor is the artiste who is naturally gifted in character and situation portrayal. A natural actor, especially after having acquired some experience through guided training and practice, brings more originality and ease to a performance than a "regulation" actor. A regulation actor could tackle a role with skill and perfection according to the rules and specifications. His performance would be appreciated as being technically accurate, but that flair and charm which distinguishes a knowledgeable natural actor may be missing. However, we are not passing value judgement on the two qualities of acting. Such a judgment would depend on the role that is being portrayed, and on the taste and sensitivity of the audience. What is important is for us to realise that an actor could be born as well as made through training and exposure.

Whether "regulation" or "natural" some actors are what is called "typecasts." A typecast is an actor whose charisma and style of acting make him/her stereotype, that is, streamlined for only a fixed type of character portrayal like an old man or woman, a bohemian, a bully, a clown, etc. Typecasts have limited opportunities for constant casting in plays. But they are generally unsurpassable in their type roles. A versatile actor has greater opportunities on stage. Because of his flexibility, he could fit into any role with conviction given an adequate touch of make-up and an appropriate voice texture where necessary. Typecasts are made by their peculiar temperaments, facial and other physical features, fixed voice textures and other natural attributes and mannerisms.

Still talking of actors, there are two primary types of actors coinciding with the two primary dramatic types: tragedy and comedy. These two primary types are the tragedian (female, tragedienne), and comedian (female, comedienne). They are not exactly typecasts in the sense of straight jacket one-role-acting, since a versatile tragedian or comedian could fit into various tragic or comic roles respectively. A tragedian/tragedienne is an actor who by temperament, features, and other natural attributes excels in serious roles but seems unconvincing if seen trying out a comic role. Conversely a comedian/comedienne by the same qualities excels in comic roles. Whereas the deportment alone of a comedian/comedienne could excite ripples of amusement, the deportment of a tragedian/tragedienne on stage could grip the audience with tremors of anxiety. Nevertheless there are specially gifted actors who could carry off tragic roles with the same convincing ease and flourish as they would use in comic roles, given appropriate make-up.

Quite often performing on stage can be an inset fun for the actor, especially where the performers have come to enjoy their roles and cooperate as a co-performers. There cannot be any inset fun (private to the actors in exclusion of the audience) unless the actors are relaxed in a performance. The more relaxed the performance becomes, the greater will the audience be relaxed and appreciative. Relaxation here does not in any way suggest looseness rather, handling a role with ease of affectation. But you should be careful about the type of fun that could constitute an eyesore before the audience, or possibly cause embarrassment. This type of misapplied actors' fun is usually noticed among beginning and amateur actors. For instance, imagine yourself acting opposite a born clown who while on stage by design or mannerism creates diversionary fun that could titillate fellow actors involuntarily. Under such circumstances some actors on stage have been seen to be laughing at the inset fun when the situation at that moment of a play demands the opposite show of mood from them. There are other distractions that could put one into a mood (especially laughter) that is wrong for a given moment in a play. As much as stage is make-believe and fun, we must try to leave the spontaneous outbursts of amusement to the audience alone, and only indulge in such hilarities or other moods as are specifically prescribed in the script or approved by the director. Should you be overwhelmed by an urge to laugh at an unprescribed fun while on stage, you are advised to suppress it by all means. If it starts getting out of hand, bite your tongue or lip until you feel pain. Although drama is make believe, we always want the audience to see a good performance as the simulation of real life circumstances until the final curtain. Should you break the spell by irrelevant or distracting behaviour, you are ruining the appreciation of the audience as well as your reputation and that of your troupe.

Artiste Temperament

To be successful in a role, the actor must totally immerse himself/herself into a given character. This calls for a process of personality transformation. That is to say the actor allows the personality of the character in the play to temporarily displace his own personality. This character substitution could have a residual psychic influence on the personality of the impersonator. The rare phenomenon occurs more where an emotive actor has to impersonate a psychopathic or an extraordinarily domineering character for several performances running. By the time the show is dead the actor may in many ways become living prototype of the character in the play. Generally the cumulative effect on an actor of extrinsic psychical influences results in the unusual personality disposition called "artiste temperament"~ a whimsical off-stage disposition which makes the non-initiates call stage personalities "mad" fellows. This capricious temperament is also noticeable in other creative and performing artists outside the stage who are often psychically involved in creativity or interpretation.

The phenomenon of "artiste temperament" is nothing strange in African traditional theatre. In Africa there are more powerful incidences of personality displacement during certain folk theatre performances, such as when an actor is required to impersonate a spirit (supernatural, ancestral, elemental, animal, metaphysical). In African societies spirits (good or evil) are ascribed superlunary personalities and temperaments. Whenever such a spirit is to be made manifest for one form of associationship with humans or the other, it is given a physical representation impersonated by a costumed actor or a human medium. Such an actor or medium has to display the prescribed or ascribed personality traits of the spirit being manifested. This presupposes that the actor should know such ascribed characteristics of the spirit-personality. And for the performance to be a successful exhibition, the actor or medium has to surrender his/her psyche to be taken over by the personality of the embodied spirit. There occurs, therefore, a process of psychical personality displacement aided by the potency of music, mask, costume, dance, charm, invocation, medication, etc. as may be required. The psychical possession of the actor by the metaphysical personality may get out of hand and require remedial treatment, such as the breaking of an egg on the forehead of the mask during the performance, in order to avert performance catastrophe. At other times exorcism of the spirit from the medium in addition to other post-performance medication to restore the actor's own personality becomes necessary. In effect then, a manifested spirit that can no longer be contained by the personality of the actor could commit unprescribed acts that could be disastrous to persons or the celebration itself; while a medium who is not attended to or exorcised immediately after an unusual demonstration of spirit possession or psychical transformation could suffer residual mental bruise, such that could make him/her seem queer. Nevertheless traditional mediums/impersonators are known to acquire unusual temperaments and personalities as they continue to be cast in such roles.

With stage artists what we witness are milder versions of acquired "artiste temperament" when compared with what obtains in our traditional circumstances. In some of our African traditional societies as well as in contemporary world societies, allowances are made by the society, generally, for the whimsical temperaments of stage personalities. The phenomenon of "artiste temperament" could be a creditable manifestation of the arrival of a stage personality as a person of elevated psychical perception.

Not everybody is used as a medium or impersonator in our traditional communion with the metaphysical forces. There should be a recognisable inherent psychic disposition in the individual. In the same way, gifted artists (stage, film, music, plastic, dance, etc.) ordinarily exhibit psychic dispositions which could develop as they become increasingly absorbed in creative or performance activities. But all artists are normal people except that they experience extra spiritual sensitivity.

To strike a balance, a good actor is expected to endow the character he/she is impersonating with something of his/her own personality. Of course this is inevitable and accounts for the fact that no two seasoned actors will give the same interpretations to a given character in a play even when given the same director, co-actors and other performance conditions. The extent to which an actor is permitted to invest his own personality on a given character-personality is usually controlled by the director of the play.

Elements of Good Acting

We generally talk of good and poor acting. These are relative aesthetic evaluations which largely depend on the tastes as well as the background of each member of the audience. However, for an average mature audience there are certain criteria for assessing the performance of any artiste as well as aesthetic levels.

1. *Stage Presence*

One of the fundamental elements of good acting is stage presence. Stage presence implies that the actor is credible and confident in a role, i.e., he/she is convincing as the character he/she is impersonating. It also implies being in full control of all of ones emotions and motions. From what we have earlier discussed we already know that there are typecasts as well as versatile actors. Whether typecast or versatile it is important in the interest of the actor as well as the production that the actor is given a role in which he/she is convincing on a visual impression. For instance it would be ridiculous to cast a maiden with uncomely features and a coarse masculine voice as the dainty maiden character in a play whom many other male actors in the play have to pine away or scheme and fight against one another to win. The audience impression on her first appearance would be negative. Their reaction would be: "She is not worth it." And thereafter they would remain unimpressed by any amount of excellent acting that goes into the entire show. Casting for a play is a most important task which the director or producer and the stage manager have to undertake with great caution and firmness. Realistic casting marks the beginning of the success of a production. Quite often in amateur production situations some artists clamour for certain roles especially principal roles, without consideration for, first of all, their visual and physical qualifications for the part. The writer recalls several instances when he was forced to bluntly tell over-ambitious artistes that they would constitute an embarrassment to themselves and the plays in the parts they were grumbling for. And nothing so offends an audience as a misfit. The audience does not want to be made to feel sorry for an actor on the grounds of physical or visual inadequacy in a part. Whether as typecasts or versatile actors, there are roles that naturally and physically become certain actors and not others. A director takes full responsibility for his casting of a play and should not allow sentiments to cloud his vision in the exercise. We cannot over-emphasize the maxim that the success of a production is greatly enhanced by convincing casting.

Having been given a suitable role, whether as a refuse collector or the president of a country, the actor has to prepare to announce his presence by studying the characteristics of such a given personality type. For this study the actor uses real life samples as well as the prescriptions in the play script. These should be blended and touched up with his own personal flair. By the time the actor is entering the stage, his demeanour will radiate the personality he is impersonating.

2.*Movement*

Acting relies on studied and stylized movements designed to communicate and signify intentions, moods and habits to fellow actors and the audience alike. Thus choreography is a specialized discipline of the theatre studies which is concerned with the study and composition of dance and movement. In our traditional theatre there are lots of accomplished and imaginative choreographers. But in our modem theatre in Nigeria, trained and capable choreographers are yet to emerge. Meanwhile most Directors have had to fulfil that role as credibly as their limited knowledge of the discipline allows, though quite often with impressive results.

Eloquent movement is, therefore, another element of good acting. A nervous or incompetent actor easily fidgets, and makes clumsy and often distracting or embarrassing movements while on stage irrespective of the directions he has received. Moods, situations and the implications of the dialogue call for various studied and significant movements which amplify the spoken word as well as the unspoken implications of a situation. Good acting requires that the actor takes trouble and pains to plot his movements and expressions under the guidance of the director who is the eyes and ears of the audience during the rehearsals. Stylized movement exercises before a rehearsal or performance helps to relax and limber up stage performers.

3. *Voice Production*

Good diction is an essential qualification for a good stage performance. A popular actor usually has a flexible vocal range and voice texture. The actor has to study the mood and character of his/her lines, underline words, phrases and lines that need special interpretation, to be stressed, to be taken faster or slower, that require change of tone QG texture or voice level or inflection. If it is a lengthy speech, the actor mark~ the pauses - whether for breath or for interpretative effect. These he does under the guidance of the director before or during rehearsals.

The most important aspect of audio-acting is distinct articulation. We have already said that on stage the dialogue and the action must be balanced to achieve good performance results. When members of the audience fail to understand what an actor is saying, they easily become irritated and may express their irritation in manners that could disconcert the actor. An actor must not throw away his lines. At every moment of vocal acting, the actor must be conscious of the fact that he must be heard by every member of a well behaved audience. Otherwise the actor easily loses credit no matter his other proficiencies as an actor. For large halls or acoustically "dead" performance venues, there are techniques for voice projection that ensure that the actor does not lose his/her voice through mere shouting. Voice projection does not imply shouting. Unless specifically prescribed for effect in certain passages of a play, it is irritating to the audience. It must be discouraged as an alternative to adequate voice projection in cases of poor acoustics or a large audience. An audience that strains too hard to pick up what is being said as a result of an actor's poor voice production could become justifiably nasty. Imagine the shock you could get when at your moment of total absorption in portraying a role somebody from the back of the audience yells: "Louder!" Or, you see and hear somebody in the middle row turn to his neighbour to ask not too softly "what is she saying"? Whenever you are on stage and notice that you are competing with restlessness and noise from the audience assess your performance. Either the play is poor, or you are delivering it poorly one way or the other, given a reasonable audience.

A good actor is acclaimed and loved by any audience and is sought after by producers and directors as a box-office attraction. What we have given are some of those elements which a beginning actor has to bear in mind right from the first moments of his/her stage experiences and development. With proper attention to these elements, and given a good play backed by a competent and imaginative director, the credit, of being a top actor i.e., a stage star, which is the dream of any stage artiste could be snatched by any moderately gifted but painstaking actor.

Above all, a good actor has to communicate very effectively all the feelings that he/she is required to experience in a play. This can be called empathic acting. Your laughter will be so infectious that the audience will chortle with you. Your happiness must so glow that the audience will feel the warmth of it. Your depressions or grief must be so touching that the audience will involuntarily commiserate you. Your annoyance has to be so real that the audience will automatically approve your reasons for that state of mind; your tenderness so palpable that it will soothe every heart in the audience. Your weeping, sobbing, or crying should seem so genuine that every member of the audience will sigh in sympathy. Your perturbation, tenor or prescribed nervousness should be so realistic that the audience will be on edge. Your clowning or your prescribed stupidity must be so artful that the audience will laugh in admiration, not in derision.

4. *Control of the Emotions*

To achieve the qualifies mentioned above the actor has to have a grip on his/her emotions. It is a very difficult assignment to laugh genuinely when you are emotionally disturbed by causes extraneous to your stage presence. It is not at all easy to weep and shed tears when, inwardly, you are feeling bright and breezy. Yet on stage nobody is interested in your private disposition before going on stage. Such a disposition must not intrude on your stage presence. A good actor therefore has to develop the capability for simulating changes of mood.

A good actor is like an accomplished liar. All other qualities taken for granted, a good liar would make a more successful actor than a person without guile. An accomplished liar never "carries his heart on his face." He is convincingly saying one thing with his expressions and voice while his inner consciousness is experiencing the opposite of the emotion he is communicating. If such a person does not apply his whole faculties into projecting the false feelings, he is easily detected - exposed by an uncontrolled expression (physical, facial or vocal). He succumbs to a natural, subconscious tendency to act in opposition to a spoken falsehood. So it is with play acting. There are poor liars and poor actors (saying something without knowing that your entire being is portraying your falsity). There are, similarly, natural liars and natural actors, skilled liars and skilled actors, convincing liars and convincing actors.

The common denominator is that accomplished actors and liars have capabilities for simulating empathy in a given situation. In our traditional societies, mourners (especially professional mourners) are known to be good actors. They can be seen crying with apparently genuine emotions in empathy with the bereaved, and the next moment they are enjoying a joke with appropriate genuine hilarity, only taking the trouble to keep an unembarrassing distance from the bereaved. So it is with acting. A good actor is skilled in evoking and portraying with empathy emotions which are not personal to him/her.

In order to acquire the skill for emotional jugglery some exercises[3] are necessary as class events and/or as personal homework before a mirror. A large sized mirror in the bedroom is an essential property which as an aspiring actor you must possess. You will find it most useful for practising and studying and co-ordinating your expressions, your moods and your comportment. Store your impressions for the stage when you can no longer see yourself but have acquired the skill of selecting and conveying any of your studied expressions etc. In any human undertaking practice makes perfect.

Exercises

Here are a few exercises for you to try out either as a class or in your private practical work.

1. ***Smile:*** Think of something really pleasant happening to you. If you are feeling it, you should be smiling. Keep the smile for about two minutes. Concentrate and study your features in a minor while you smile. Stop. Now think of something distasteful, and as you are reliving its experience in your imagination try to smile. You might notice that before half a minute you are no longer smiling but grinning. Note the difference between the two. Smiling lights up the face and eyes while a grin is a mere show of teeth that looks silly - like what you see on a roasted goat head. Your eyes will be dull.

    If you can see the difference, then concentrate on trying the smiling exercise a couple more times. Each time try to consciously keep the smile for a longer period. Say, imagine that you are in the presence of someone you love very dearly, and that you are trying to charm the person with your smile through which you are communicating the

---

[3] Some examples *for* class or individual practices will be included, where necessary as illustrations or guides.

intensity of your love. The smile is the most brilliant and beautiful expression the face can achieve. Whenever you are on stage, keep a pleasant thought handy for your smiling scenes just in case your co-actor fails to inspire such a feeling in you.

Grinning might be prescribed on stage in circumstances where you are required to pretend an amusement which you do not feel. When you grin, whether as a result of pain, or stiff or false amusement, remember that your eyes do not light up as in a smile. Grinning is a stupid—4ooking showing of the teeth and is very irritating to an onlooker.

2.   **Chuckle:** A chuckle is suppressed laughter which rumbles in the throat and bursts through the lips in involuntary spurts. When a person is genuinely chuckling he/she should notice his/her shoulders, upper stomach muscles and throat quaking slightly while the eyes will be dancing with merriment.

3.   **Laughter:** For this exercise it is recommended that members of the class stand up and away from their seats. It is best taken in an empty space. Laughter is probably more difficult to achieve than a smile or a chuckle. Quite often on stage people produce empty, lifeless, irritating sounds that are supposed to go for laughter - something sounding like "Ha-ha-ha". "Ha-ha-ha" is only an expression that sounds the way it is written and could imply derision or drab amusement. Genuine laughter is a brilliant sound that is full of soul and warms the heart of a listener. It comes from full chest, not a constricted throat that produces the "ha-ha-ha" sound. In a standing position, let the class begin to laugh and continue to laugh up to a point of tears, hysteria and collapse. Once again it might be useful to remember any amusing incident that really made you laugh and which always makes you laugh when you remember it irrespective of where you may be.

If the laughter exercise is properly done, you will discover that you have undergone several involuntary movements which should take you away from your original position. You will be unsteady on your feet, may fall around, knock against furniture, grope and grab for support. Just let yourself go, and keep laughing until tear drops being to form and flow, until you are reeling on the ground beating your palms and holding your ribs. Keep laughing until you are exhausted and grasping for breath. Genuine laughter exhausts, but it does give a healthy feeling by the time you are exhausted and groaning. Genuine laughter is an enjoyable sound issuing from your soul which an audience anywhere loves to hear. Unfortunately it is hard to come by in real life. You will be surprised to observe that you can go through a week or a couple of weeks without meeting anybody laughing genuinely. It might be interesting to run a class competition on laughter.

In order to identify the three examples of amusement given above, combine the three exercises. Start with a smile and let the smile develop freely into chuckles, and allow the chuckle to explode into a merry laugh, and keep laughing until you end up chuckling again and finally smiling as a result of the refreshed feeling you are experiencing.

4. **Disgust:** Disgust is not always expressed in sound. It could be effectively registered as a facial expression which screws up your features and is often supplemented with a brisk movement of the hand. You must really feel disgusted before ever you can register it effectively on your features.

5. **Anger:** When a person is angry, his blood pressure rises. His heart beats faster. His eyes are fierce and fiery. He is highly tensed up and more often than not he exhibits some activity which is a physical extension of his aroused temper. If he tries to suppress the anger from exploding into action, the effort is easily noticeable in the stiffening of the body and the features and the tense clasping of the fist or any other handy object. Suppressing intense anger

can be a disastrous exercise and is therefore more dangerous than allowing it to explode.

An angry person requires a physical outlet, an activity that will explode and drain him of his tenseness, and lower his blood pressure. Otherwise he could burst a vein - and some people do burst their veins at moments of intense anger. The eyes are the most eloquent indicators of the magnitude of anger a person is experiencing. The face becomes taut, the veins stand visibly out, and the entire body stiffens. The physical emission of anger depends on the occasion as well as the temperament of the individual. If the person is speaking, the texture or tone of the voice changes, and the rate of speech gets faster or slower depending on the nature of the person. Either way the voice becomes tense, rises in pitch, and is on edge. At other times there could be one form of physical action or the other determined by the cause and circumstances of the anger, the sitting, lying or standing position as well as the physical environment of the person.

On some occasions, depending on how the provocation comes, one may have to allow the intensity of anger to build up to a climax. That is the moment of utmost control which is marked by vocal or physical outburst. Fast or heavy breathing and flared nostrils are other physiological manifestations of anger. For a built-up anger the rate of breathing helps to measure the mounting intensity of provocation. An actor should always make a mental note of occasions in ordinary life when he/she has experienced great anger. Better still he should mentally document various causes of anger as well as his feelings, expressions and motive reactions for each type of annoyance. Thus on stage it becomes useful to recall, and transport one's psychic self into the appropriate angry occasion in order to stimulate the feelings.

Other useful exercises should include short practical demonstrations of Tiredness, Bewilderment, Shock, Surprise, Fed-upness, Fear, Crying, Physical pain, Disappointment, etc.

A recommended technique for the practice of emotional expression is to have the teacher or one's rehearsal partner tell an anecdote that should elicit any of the emotions, and have the class or individual simulate the emotional reactions desired. (Appropriate passages from plays or novels would equally be suitable) Some examples:

1. Imagine that as a job seeker you attended an interview for a position you very much wanted to secure. You are well qualified for the job. Nonetheless, you had prepared yourself for the interview. At the interview you were convinced you answered all the questions brilliantly and could sense that you impressed the interview panel who in turn gave you reasons to hope that you satisfied them. You were told by the Chairman to expect their letter. There were two vacancies while only three of you were called for the interview.

   Back home, you were so confident that you privately imagined yourself as a wage earner very soon. You may have even hinted to your parents and close associates about your bright prospects for the job. Then a letter arrives bearing the stamp of the establishment that interviewed you.

   (a) Receive the letter... .(What feelings are you experiencing on receiving the letter? - *Anxiety* and *Hope?* Let your feelings show on your face, hands)

   (b) Now you begin to open the envelop. (Are you nervous and fumbling? As you open the envelop and extract the folded letter does the envelop drop off your hands, ignored?)

   (c) Now you unfold the letter ... (Are your hands steady/ Are you biting your lower lip? Are you holding your breath for the confirmation of the most important news in your life - the offer of appointment, getting a much longed for job?)

   (d) Now you read the contents (aloud).. "We regret to inform you that you were unsuccessful.."

(Disappointment! Did your voice shake and tail off as you came to the word "unsuccessful"? Where is the letter now? How are you looking - eyes transfixed, unseeing, begging for tears? How does your body feel - tired, slumpy, cold? What happened to the suspended breath?)

(e) Try to stand up and move away...

2. You are working late at night in your room. It is about 1 a.m. Everybody around you has been sleeping for a long time now. The only sound in the night is the occasional scratching of pen on paper, and turning of leaves produced by you. You live alone in your room.

You get up, leave the lights on and go out, leaving your door open. You go to the toilet.

You come back about two minutes afterwards. Your dour is now closed. Without thinking about whether you left it open or not you open the door to your room. What! It is in darkness... (How do you feel? *Puzzled?*)

The electricity company again? You hesitate a bit... "Oh well, those annoying fellows." Then while vaguely puzzling it all out you begin to grope your way into the pitch dark room to locate a box of matches on your working desk.

You hit your knee violently on the iron bed post and wince in pain emitting a sharp vocal sound of anger as you cradle the leg with two hands.

Just then there is a loud crash in the room right ahead of you... (What do you feel? *Scared?* What happens to your hands that were holding your hurt knee? What happens to your knee? What about the sharp pain you were feeling? How are you breathing?).

You hesitate, alarmed. There is no further sound. Then just as you collect yourself to move quickly to your table and the matches, a powerful beam of light from a torch dazzles your face and brain.. (How do you feel? *Alarmed? Shocked?* Do you yell? Or do you droop your mouth and pop your eyes like a dead fish - in terror?)

Five seconds..., seven, eight, ten seconds (Are you sweating? Trembling? Where are your hands and what are they trying to do? What of your face?)

Then without any warning the frightful silence is shattered by a crack of mocking laughter. The torchlight goes off, and light from the electric bulb floods your room. There ... by your desk is your prankster friend and neighbour... (How do you feel? *Relieved? Angry?*) Do you inhale and heave a mighty breath to recover your terrified faculties? Do you collapse on the bed exhausted by that short but intense terror? Or do you take up issues angrily with your friend?).

3. For you life is now hopeless. It is true you have a comfortable living and an enviable job. But the one thing that you have needed desperately -*Love* - has not been fair to you. Not long ago it finally came your way and just as you were determined to make it permanent through marriage you were informed that the one whom you love so desperately has abandoned you and gone off with a friend of yours. Imagine, just at the time you are on the threshold of formally announcing your engagement.

Then that particular day, a co-worker with whom you fell out, insults you by telling you that you can never get married because you are already too old to be wanted, and that it is the psychological cause of your tantrums. As if the news of your having been deserted by your only hope has got around, this angry co-worker tells you that anybody who pretends to love you is just fooling you. Everybody in the general office adjoining your cubicled office has a good laugh on that, at your expense.

You are so shattered, disturbed, that you leave the office and start wandering, just drifting with tormented mind. You arrive at the public park and slump down disconsolately, your head propped on your two palms. You are brooding. You've been sitting like that for you know not how long. You don't care. Time no longer exists for you. Then suddenly, as if in a dream, you become conscious of a pair of legs right in front of you ... *(Bewilderment)*. You must be imagining things. So you close your eyes, open them and through the brimming tear drops you look again... The legs are still there.

Then you start to follow the legs up with your eyes, pass the knees, up to a hip, a trunk, and finally you focus on the face. *It can't be! Surely it is hallucination.* But the face is carrying a brilliant, understanding smile. It is the face of the lover whom you were told you've lost to a friend forever... *Incredible.* You rub your eyes and rub off the tears absent-mindedly... *Cumulative shock.*

But the smiling face is still there. Oh dear, what could he/she be wanting from you now? But the smile persists and charms you.

The look on your face makes your lost love stoop towards you, concerned. You call his/her name and he/she responds by stretching out two hands towards you and saying with a voice aimed at cheering you up: "What has come over you? You thought I've left you? No my dear. It was just silly malicious gossip. As soon as I got a hint of it I went to your office. You were not there. But I finally tracked you here. Come, I will be yours forever... Or don't you want me again"?

Your lover smiles. The smile authenticates the sincerity of voice which confirmed his/her love for you... (How do you feel now? Moving from despondence to hope to happiness all coming in such quick succession? The wrinkles on your worried brow creasing out? The tear drops still lingering while your face begins to light with the smile that translates your heart as full of joy).

Then your lover says again "Come to me my dear..." (Demonstrate your response).

4. *Elocution:* Good elocution as we had earlier mentioned is a vital quality of good acting which must be acquired by an aspiring actor. Poor elocution can be improved through

training and exercises if the aspirant has other essential assets for the stage.

Voice production starts with breathing. Speech is supported and sustained with breath. Try talking while you are breathing fast. Then take a deep breath and hold it for as long as you can while talking all the time. Finally take a deep breath and exhale slowly, holding it for as long as you can without talking. You will notice that in the first exercise your speech will be disturbed - jerky and incoherent. In the second exercise your voice starts rich and thins off as you run out of breath. If you breathe immediately after and try to repeat what you said before you'll notice that you'll run out of breath faster and faster with each try. Try timing the second and third exercises, and you will observe that you sustained your breath longer when you were not talking. Talking takes up energy, and the way you breathe affects the way your speech comes out, while the emotion with which you are speaking affects your breathing.

When people are asked to take a deep breath you might notice some of them raising their shoulders and contracting their abdominal muscles.

This is not correct. The shoulder has nothing to do with breathing and should never really move when one is taking a proper breathing exercise. And whenever you contract your abdominal muscles you are driving air out instead of inviting it into your body. For a proper breathing exercise allow your abdominal muscles to relax and expand. Your diaphragm drops. The cavity enclosed by the ribs and intercostal muscles within which your lungs are encased then automatically expands. A partial vacuum is now created inside you. The natural tendency is for air to rush in to fill your lungs, thereby expanding them to fill up the partial vacuum. Exhale slowly and evenly making a vowel sound and listening intently for any change in tone or level which would suggest irregular exhalation. If you push too hard on articulation of the sound you'll force out most of the air, and not only will you run out of breath too fast, you will notice that the sound you arc producing becomes thin and forced too soon. A good actor takes time to study the phrasing of his/her lines, marking points at which to pause and breathe.

For voice production the following organs of the human body are vital: Breath from the lungs supplies and sustains the intensity of the speech sound; the larynx-throat makes the sound; the mouth cavity resonates the sound while the lips help it to shape the sound. When we talk of voice production on stage we have certain techniques of speech in mind. Monotonous tone and level of speech are tiresome to the audience and could make them yawn and fall asleep. An actor who starts a sentence and fades into inaudibility towards the end is equally a nuisance. The first syllable of a sentence is as important as its last syllable. Good public speaking implies that the speaker articulates distinctly and audibly all the syllables of his/her lines. This is not to recommend over-articulating of words or of consonant sounds which are very offensive on stage.

As much as possible use your natural voice level. Chest voice is throaty and harsh, and would not carry far. Highly pitched head voice would sound thin and unnatural (falsetto). The power in your voice is supplied by good breathing and proper sounding of the vowels using the mouth cavity as a megaphone. In a large auditorium with a large audience and poor acoustics remember that human beings, their dresses and hair absorb sound. You will therefore require an extra lift to your voice to project up to the last row in the auditorium. It is better to acquire this extra lift during rehearsals. And it is a skill that comes with proper and constant practice. Don't depend on trying to shout down the audience. You will sound hoarse. You will exhaust yourself. You might even lose your voice by the time the show is over. An actor who constantly loses his/her voice as a result of poor voice production is an unreliable investment and will be unpopular with directors.

For a distant projection, push the sound towards your upper palate aiming for the resonating chamber around your nose. If you are doing it properly and place a finger on either side of your nose, you will feel the vibration of the sound. Use vowel sound during this exercise. You most be careful in this exercise not to speak through the nose. Nasalised speech coming from an actor on stage is nauseating. You will notice that when you make the same sounds with your chest voice, the vibration will stop. You must therefore continue to make a conscious effort until it becomes your stage habit to lift your voice.

Quite often you are instructed in a script or by a director to whisper, especially in conspiratorial passages. Whispering in real life is for only the ear or ears you mean to hear what you are saying. Whispering on stage is meant not only for the ear with you on stage but also for the entire audience. Even if there is another pair of ears on stage with you that should be excluded from your whisper, the director will teach you how to give the impression that the wrong ears are excluded, never the audience. Stage whispering is a technique of voice projection in which your words are articulated through the hush sound associated with whispers.

Some other times some lines are required to be said with emotional inflection of the voice: nervous voice, weeping voice, laughing voice, pained voice, angry voice, strained voice, happy voice, gushing voice, etc. Through practice, bearing in mind the sound quality of each particular emotion in life circumstances, these can be achieved on stage. Ability to achieve a range of emotions with the voice is an attribute of an accomplished actor.

When we stress good elocution on stage it is important for the actor to realise also that he/she is not merely reciting, but talking. Fluent clear conversational style, not affected reciting style of elocution is the ideal which soothes the audience, except of course in passages that require the actor to recite a poem or verse, to orate or mimic.

Finally an actor has to pay attention to the dynamics of the voice. The dynamics of elocution are suggested in the implications of the sentences, phrases and words. If the actor studies his/her lines well so that he/she expresses their meanings intelligently, instead of parroting them as syllables of a language, his/her vocal acting will be appealing to the audience. When vocal dynamics are used to effectively project the meaning or implication of sentences, phrases and words, the speaker is said to have achieved good expression, which is an important recommendation of good elocution.

For meaningful expression, attention should also be paid to tempo of speech. Most often the normal tempo of speech is what is required according to character type. But there are occasions when it becomes necessary to accelerate or retard the tempo of speech in order to achieve effects required by the script or the director in certain situations of a play. For instance, at tense moments of a play, a faster rate of speech may be called for just as in normal life; where as at didactic moments a slower rate would be more appropriate.

These are just pointers to conscious proper elocution especially for beginning actors. They become unconsciously applied techniques with practice and experience. Any actor who has studied his/her part thoroughly and is living it as if it were in his/her natural life would automatically achieve appropriate elocution and save the director a lot of trouble and rehearsal time.

5. *Characterisation:* It is characters that make a play. This implies that no two characters in a play even if they are twins can be the same person, i.e. say or do the same

things the same way, behave generally the same. A study of characterisation is a study of the totality of acting; a study of how to be a unique personality in a given play; and a different individual in different plays, a study of how to give the same reaction to the same impulses/situations with different personal touches. Each assigned character in every new play is a fresh study. For instance a tyrannical chief in play "A" is a different personality from a tyrannical chief in play "B".

Our approach to characterisation should therefore be guided exercises in personality types, situational behaviour patterns, and non-verbal communication. Although one actor's interpretation should naturally differ from another actor's interpretation of the same character, there should be common standard features of the given character in all the variations of proper interpretations.

The play script is the principal guide to character interpretation. Characters are more or less made in the script through the things they say, the things they do, and often how they do such things. What the actor does therefore is to give life and identity to the playwright's abstract stage personalities. In other words, to impersonate imaginary but defined characters. For this process of impersonation the actor employs the following elements of characterisation:

a. The physical form and features: wrinkled? bushy eyebrows? heavy eyebrows? prominent eyelids or eyelashes'? deep set eyes? squinting eyes? moustache? bearded? square faced? acquiline hose? bald headed? broad-chested? stooped? pot-belied? crooked fingers? heavy buttocks? foot drop? tall and elegant? squat and fat headed? comely? dainty? ugly? etc. etc. To achieve these elements of character distinction as might be defined, the actor's own physical form and features are his/her first qualification. Thereafter make—up and costume are used to create other features. Finally the actor's skill makes up for the rest of the prescribed physical assets of a given character.

b. Voice characterisation: stammers? lisps'? drawls? tattles? nasalises? dialectal affectation? old age affectation? heavy tongued? bellows? shrill voiced? etc. For voice characterisation the script gives the distinguishing fundamentals. The actor may use his/her natural voice, or culture or adapt his/her voice as may be required. He/she may also be require to adopt mannerisms of expression or diction.

c. Movement and mime: stiff carriage? frowning? sniffing? gesticulating widely? carries head in a peculiar manner? terrified? confused? astounded? winking? listening? bowlegged? walks with a limp? walks fast? walks heavily? walks on balls of feet? in a hurry? swings hip? shuffles? moves seductively? moves stealthily? sickly? full of energy? shaking? searching? frightened? shivering with cold? agonising with pain? lying dead? staggering with drunkenness? short-sighted? cultivating with a hoe? jubilating? collapsing with fatigue? despondent? etc.

We have already said that characterisation is a skill acquired through observation and study, and mastered through practice. We have also outlined the three factors that must be borne in mind for effective impersonation of character, *situation,* mood, attitude.

6. *Personal preparation:* It is ideal to give every actor a complete copy of a play in which he/she will be taking part. Having secured a role and a copy of the play, a diligent actor should read the play through once with an aim to understanding the story.

Read through it again, this time more slowly in order to study and understand:

(a) the character role assigned to you

(b) the other characters with whom you have to interact.

A knowledge of the characters with whom you are going to deal as contained in the play would help you in interpreting your part. In interpreting your part you should adopt the following approaches:

(i) Who are you? What are the written implications of your personality? These implications can be found:

  (a) in the lines you have to say

  (b) in the stage directions concerning your activities, and

  (c) in what the other characters have to say about you in the play.

(ii) What are the expressions that could help you in the portrayal of your role? Once again hints about these expressions can be found in:

  (a) the lines you have to say

  (b) the stage directions about your expressions and circumstances at any moment in the play

  (c) the interpretations or reactions and activities, according to the script or the director, which the other characters give to your expressions.

(iii) What original qualities, personal touches, can you bring to the part? Remember, as we had said earlier, that a character is created by the playwright in a play. But the way that character lives on stage varies from one actor-interpreter of the part to another. It is your personal touches in bearing, mime, elocution, movement and expressions that will determine your magnificence in your interpretation of a character. If you do not understand the role you are playing, obviously your are in no position to give an original spark to it as an actor. Your performance will then be, at the best, a mediocre achievement. Note that an effective pause, an appropriate overlap of another speaker; an eloquent sigh, sneer, pout, stare, inclination of the head, flick of the hand, throw of the hip; just the right lift or drop in your voice are examples of the subtle details that distinguish star actors. And they are usually learned and deliberate artistic and aesthetic details that embellish ordinary acting.

7.   *Stage Movement:* Stage movement requires skill. It is an art, an accomplishment which has to be consciously acquired and skillfully executed. Any stage artiste, in order to become distinguished, must in addition to proper elocution and charm of expressions demonstrate sensitivity of judgment in movement. It is an eyesore to witness an actor executing uncertain or awkward movements on stage during a performance. Even where an awkward movement is prescribed, it has to be skillfully executed. But generally, be a leopard, NOT an elephant in your movements on stage.

Beginning exercises in stage movement should be aimed at curing flat-footedness and natural clumsiness. Attention should be paid to the flowing strides effected by using the balls of your feet for leverage like a dancer. Group exercises on walking should be encouraged as one of the preliminary warm-ups before rehearsals.

Exercises on proper stepping could go with balancing exercises. Balance for a few counts as you rise on each foot. Slow sustained movements are better for these exercises. The hands should be kept in various stationary positions during the exercises: sideways stretched; upwards stretched carrying an imaginary globe; lifting an imaginary basket at various levels; palms on the head; downwards stretched; akimbo; folded across the chest; linked behind, below the buttocks; alternate forward and backward movements as in normal walking but with sustained or fast swings.

For another exercise on balancing, stand on a spot, heels together. Rise slowly on the balls of your feet pause for a count of seven as you achieve maximum height. Then, still standing on the balls of your feet go down into a squatting position, heels together, knees sideways, head erect, chest out, stomach in, buttocks in. Balance on the balls of your feet in the squatting position for another slow count of seven, then rise slowly to a standing position. Various hand positions as in the preceding exercise should be used, and each exercise should be tried two or three times. Exercises on walking and balancing must be done without any shoes on.

In the above exercise and any others you may try out, always keep your head up and your chin out. The position of your head when you are on stage is very important. Keep your head up always. This establishes your self-confidence and stage presence. It also assists in proper voice production. Don't ever look on the floor unless you are especially required to look on the floor, say, to demonstrate a shy village maiden for instance. Then do it where it is stipulated and no more. Speaking or looking towards the floor is a sure sign of an actor who is scared of the audience.

In proscenium type theatre you are to remember, always, that you *Never* back your audience unless you are specifically directed so to do. In theatre-in-the-round type however, this cannot be helped. The director and actors will then plan movements such that no section of the audience is backed all the time.

A movement called "crossing the stage" is one in which an actor moves with the wrong hand or leg, thereby presenting an awkward picture. Crossing the stage can unbalance you. Try as a matter of practice to use the right hand or leg to initiate or execute, as the case may be, all movements towards your right; and the left hand or leg for all movements towards your left. Note also that whenever you are required to turn into the scene or the audience, or to turn away from the scene or the audience, as the case may be, the smallest angle of turn is the proper turning movement. In doing so, make sure not to cross your legs or you could trip and fall. If you are facing the left stage wall for instance, and you are required to turn and face the audience, it would be crass stupidity to attempt to accomplish the turn by your left thereby executing a 270 degrees turning circle and backing the audience in the process. If from the same position you want to turn into the scene to face the right stage wall, the proper direction is the 180 degrees turning circle through your right i.e., the audience side. Although turning through your left is an equal turning circle, a left turn would make you back the audience in other words always treat the back stage wall as the wall that it is. Never face it while you are on stage unless it is specifically recommended; and never execute movements that will make you face it no matter how briefly, unless you are again specifically required or directed to do so.

There are moments on stage when you are left idling. That is those moments when no speech or acting is assigned to you. Those could be difficult moments for an actor when he/she could look stupid if he or she has no stage presence or experience. The password for such idling movements is: "look part of the scene." Take interest in what is going on around you; using your eyes, your ears, appropriate mime and movement. At such moments your reaction to what is happening might be the cue that would guide the audience as to how to take the message. It is better to get lost from the stage than to look lost on stage. On the other hand, you must avoid movements that would call undue attention to you, thereby diverting attention from the focus of event i.e., whoever is talking or is supposed to be the centre of activity at any moment. If you do that, you will be cheating your co-actors. You will be a nuisance because you will be distracting the audience from the more important thing going on at those particular moments. Never call undue attention to yourself. You would be playing to the gallery by so doing. And that is an uncomplimentary expression to be applied to an artiste. If you solicit undue notice you could ruin the particular scene although you might earn irrelevant audience notice in the form of laughter, derision or outright disapproval. On the other hand never hide when you should be seen. Soliciting undue attention and hiding yourself are examples of poor acting, or signs of nervousness. When you are idling, rather than make stupid or distracting movements, stay quiet and make yourself inconspicuous. That would be more tolerable although not advisable. Tied to these is overacting. Somebody overacting on stage can be compared to a busybody in ordinary life. Precise movements and expressions executed the right way and at the right moments are all that are required of an accomplished actor. Superfluous movements and expressions, or outright aimless or useless movements and expressions spotlight poor and immature acting.

Bear in mind that the acting area is a space that has been designated for stage activity. Always aim at filling the space with your presence through activities. But you are at the same time to apply caution in filling the stage so that you do not execute distracting or meaningless movements, especially the type that could detract from, instead of enhance what you may be saying.

Balance (in space, action, elocution) is essential at all times on stage. Balance also includes balance in roles. At every moment when there are actors on stage, somebody must be the focus and that centre or focus of activity should be the speaker except where the speaker's function is that of providing a commentary on other vital stage activities.

By now you must have noticed that the stage is a place where you are required to do something well or not at all. For a beginning actor it means that you have many things to think about at the same time. You are bound to make mistakes. You should not be shy about making these mistakes. It is only by correction and practice that you will overcome your initial difficulties until going on stage becomes you. That is the time when you simply do the right thing the right way without thinking too much about it. When you have acquired this skill you can appropriately be called an actor.

8. *Handling Your Audience:* There are times in a performance when the audience becomes difficult, or an outright nuisance. At such times an actor wishes himself/herself kilometres away from the stage. If your show is of poor quality (whether in material or presentation or both) then you asked for it, and there is little that can be done to bail you out. If on the other hand the audience is distractingly appreciative of your superb show, or simply noisy for reasons not of your own making, there are subtle ways of attempting to control them from your stage advantage.

For a noisy audience, an experienced actor can improvise as part of his/her dialogue an appeal or order for silence. This is usually given in a voice that should surprise the audience into attentiveness. If you are successful, do not pause to celebrate your achievement, or to exhibit your disapproval of the audience's attitude. Rather, continue with your performance as if what you accomplished was merely part of your show that served another useful function. The following fill-up examples suggest patterns that could be effective in hushing your audience. But you must introduce whatever fill-up you use at appropriate spots in your dialogue; that, is where experience comes in useful.

(i) Listen!... I said, Listen to me!!" "Now pay attention!...
     Pay attention to what I am going to say!..."
(ii) "Silence!! ... Silence everywhere!!"
(iii) You: *(to the audience)* Hey! Are you hearing me?
     'Did you hear what I said"
     Audience. YES! NO!
     You: Then Listen...

Whichever version you use or formulate would be determined by the nature of what you were saying and whom you were addressing on stage at that particular moment. Take a deep breath and project towards the back row of the audience which is where noise-making and other forms of disturbances usually start because of its disadvantageous or advantageous (for noise-making) distance from the stage. You could back up your voice with appropriate movements. But never lose your head because of the uncooperative attitude of the audience. You will merely assist them in spoiling everything if you exhibit perturbation, impatience or rudeness.

Another effective technique for calming a noisy audience is to suddenly raise your voices level above normal pitch. But do not shout, or if it calls for shouting, don't keep the loud voice for more than a line or two if the trick fails to work. Otherwise you may strain your voice. The psychology of this technique is that when you suddenly raise your voice, the audience receives the subtle message that you have something very important for them to hear.

An audience gets noisy when members become bored or uneasy, or when they fail to pick your words from all sides of the hall. To insure against embarrassment from an audience, don't take chances with the following pieces of advice:

a. Choose your plays well, keeping your audience type in mind. But remember that it is also your duty to help the audiences progressively expand or improve their taste. By this we mean that you should give them what is good and will interest them, but not necessarily what they want to see because it is the type and₁ standard/they are used to. J

b. Prepare your production well. Give spirited acting. Avoid allowing the play to drag in the middle. Choose and maintain a tempo suitable to the mood and style of the play. Given a suitable, well-produced and performed play, the audience usually hushes and controls itself.

c. Make adequate arrangement for seating your audience comfortably. The more crowded and uncomfortable an audience, the more its propensity to be restless, thereby ruining your play through disturbances.

d. Do not waste time during scene changes. Use easy to move stage sets and props even if they have to look simple. If there is need for an intermission, then let the audience take their break at the scheduled point in the play.

e   Make sure your words carry to all sides of the hall. In a good production, noise generally starts when members of the audience start asking their neighbours what an actor has said that produced an articulated response from the audience. Or when those at the back rows begin to heckle you with requests like, *"Louder Please."*

An effective device if your protagonist's line is lost either during an applause or noise, or because he/she failed to project well enough (and the line is important for your rejoinder) is to incorporate his/her line in yours. That is, you announce or repeat such an important lead in indirect speech form before taking your rejoinder to it. This technique is equally useful when your co-actor suddenly has a blackout and forgets his/her line. If he/she jumps cue and lands at the wrong section of the dialogue, it is a saving device to bring him/her back to the right point by introducing his/her proper cue line, indirectly, before taking yours.

Example:

X: Meet me at the railway station tomorrow by 6 p.m. I will deliver the goods then.

Y: The time would not be safe. There could be many people around. Why not later, at night, say 10 p.m.

X: That suits me. Bye for now.

Exit

X.

Now, supposing X's first lines are lost either in the noise of the audience or because the voice did not carry well. Or supposing X forgot what to say and is about to look lost; or supposing he jumped such an important lead and goes to another sequence in the play. Since his first line is an important cue to subsequent sequences, Y should incorporate Xs lines by announcing its substance as follows:

X: (lines lost)

Y: Oh, you want to deliver the goods to me by 6 p.m. tomorrow at the railway station? I'm afraid that time wouldn't be safe. There could etc.

Every actor should be able to differentiate between audience disturbance and audience appreciation. Of course every actor wants to feel the pulse of audience appreciation during his/her performances, because it helps to give spark to the quality of an actor's performance. But there are times when audience appreciation becomes a nuisance, such as at moments when a pause to allow such appreciation to subside would ruin the tempo and tension of a dialogue exchange. Rather than lose your feeling for the passage, keep the pace of your dialogue regardless of the disturbance. It is better that the audience suffers the penalty for being over emotional or over enthusiastic than that you drop out of mood. Experience has shown that when the audience discovers that their applause is debarring them from following a fast and exciting passage in a performance its members instinctively hush or restrain themselves. Light-hearted plays like comedy and farce do at times make allowances for applause or laughter as a structural sequence in the production. In more serious plays like tragedy or melodrama, to pause and accommodate excess audience exuberance could ruin the overall effectiveness of certain passages.

We are not however insisting on any hard or rigid solutions to the relationship between an actor and the audience. For experienced actors every given situation should suggest its own emergency remedy. What is important is that an actor should know his/her typical audience behaviour. A good knowledge of your audience is as important as your adequate preparation for a performance. With that, you will avoid being surprised, shocked, embarrassed or intimidated by your audience. Imagine how you would feel the day after, if your individual performance, or your group's presentation as a whole is booed and thereby adjudged a failure by the audience, members of which you will confront in your every day life as you move into the society.

More Exercises on Acting

a. There are qualities, mannerisms and attitudes which identify certain professional, occupational, social or ethnic groups of people. Playwrights usually draw from character types within their experiences. Thereafter they can imbue such character-types with special qualities or personalities depending on the ability of the playwright and his mode of writing.

We have talked of typecasts as actors who specialise in impersonating specific human or character types. Since acting generally is impersonation of "man in Society" by gifted impersonators (actors), exercises in characterisation are necessary as part of your practical drama education.

The first step in characterisation is a study of character types. We are going to list some character types within your experiences that have distinguishable attitudinal patterns, each as a group. You will be required to list the qualities and mannerisms of deportment, speech or social interaction which typify each group. For instance:

A typical "Been-to" lady: very self-conscious; affectation of intonation in speech in order to sound English; always sits with leg crossed above the knee; openly snobs her background by reminding her listeners about her experiences abroad e.g. "when I was in

England....", calls attention to her dresses and make up in public by fidgeting about or with them; moves with short brisk steps even within a short distance; carries herself with self-conscious air of importance; generally fussy and affectations.

Now try to list the typifying qualities of each of the following character types:

A typical school principal (your own principal). An officious school prefect (the one in your school). A student who is too conscious of his wealthy background. The swot. The bully. The truckpusher. The policeman. The taxi driver. The office messenger. The politician. The busybody. The drama director. The tyrant. The village woman. The civil servant. The school cook. The flirt. The catechist. The gossip. The stammerer. The medical doctor. The trader.

Maybe you have always taken the above character types for granted. This is now an opportunity for you to pay closer attention to the behaviour patterns of people around you. A promising artist (actor, musician, costumier, painter, writer, dancer) should develop a keen sense of observation. Everything that happens around you should be observed with an eye for details and peculiarities. For the actor it is these peculiarities which he/she has stored up consciously or subconsciously that are selectively called up in character portrayal. At other times it is helpful to model your interpretation of your part in a play on a living prototype whom you know very well.

b. The next step is to try out short anecdotes: speech, movement, mannerism, behaviour, carriage of the character types you have written up. Every student should take his/her turn in these short character sketches. One approach to the exercise would be to have a student portray a character he/she has sketched and let the class identify the character type or the particular individual so impersonated.

c. Class exercises in mime could be based on folk tales and fables. The story should be told once or twice so that everybody would understand it. Then the characters in the story should be assigned to members of the class to act the story in mime. For this exercise it might be preferred to collect a number of short stories and divide the class into groups. Each group should then be assigned a story to work out for about ten minutes. The class would then reassemble to assess the performances of various groups.

The following are two folk stories suitable for mime activities:

(i) I came to your house. You gave me a piece of stone and called it kolanut. I made a carrier's pad and threw it outside. I then asked you to help me lift the earth to my head. You cursed me for being stupid, and querried how I could ever think that the earth could be carried. I cursed you too and asked you whether a stone has ever been broken as kolanut. You ran into your room and came out with two prizes with which we congratulated each other for matching wits.

When I was leaving you gave me a cock and instructed me that after twelve days you would come with baskets to collect its chicks. I went home, unperturbed, with the cock. After twelve days you came to my house with baskets to collect the chicks. I lamented to you that since the time I returned home my father had given birth to a baby while my mother had fallen from the top of a tall palm tree.

You threw a curse at me and asked me whether women climb any trees at all not to talk of a man giving birth to a baby - both abominations. I flung the curse back at you and inquired of you whether you've ever seen or heard of a cock laying eggs not to talk of its hatching them into chicks. Then I ran into my room and came out with two prizes with which we congratulated each other for matching wits.

(ii) Every time *Nza*, (a tiny but intelligent bird) and *Obu* (a large clumsy bird) met, *Obu* would ridicule *Nza* because of its disadvantage in size, wondering why with all the food it was forever consuming, it never improved in size. One day *Nza* was so piqued by these smarting ridicules that it decided to teach *Obu* a bitter lesson. It challenged *Obu* to a contest - a trial of stamina. It proposed that they would try a fasting contest, neither eating nor going to toilet until one of them would concede victory to the stronger party. Obu was very much amused. So with great bluff, and relying on its advantage of size it readily agreed.

Nza then located two trees within visible distance of each other, and directed *Obu* to take one as its station for the combat while it *(Nza)* would take the other. The dull-witted *Obu* agreed again with much over confidence. But it did not know that *Nza* had before that time gone and selected the two trees for special reasons: the tree which it assigned to *Obu* was infested with large hard-biting, flesh nibbling tailor ants. while the tree it had reserved for itself was colonized by small, harmless, edible ants. However each bird retired to its station and the contest started.

After a short while, during which it had had a meal on the small ants, *Nza* called across to *Obu* and proposed that they should sing at interval so that they could know how each of them was standing up to the rigours of the contest. *Obu* called back its consent to the proposal. *Nza* then instructed *Obu* to reply every time it heard *Nza* sing and to reply with the same song, to which *Obu* agreed.

Nza went back to its meal picking the small ants. On its own perch, *Obu* was busy fighting back with diminishing success the assault of the tailor ants that had invaded it as if with venom. After a good meal Nza preened itself and sang out in a brilliant merry voice:

Solo	*Chorus*
Nza and *Obu* made a pact	*nzamili*
Nza and *Obu* made a pact	
To neither eat nor toilet	

Until a victor emerges

Cho cho kwa

Cho cho kwa

Poor *Obu* contained its agony and immediately replied bravely, singing the same song with a heavy voice dulled by pain.

Nza resumed its meal; while *Obu* continued battling the onslaught of tailor ants devouring it with nibbling bites. After another appropriate interval, *Nza* would call out again in a merrier tone, while *Obu* would, bravely, call back in a progressively weakened and agonised tone of voice.

As time passed the replies from *Obu* were getting more and more feeble as it started dying slowly, not only from hunger which it could have contended with for a longer while but more from the pains of being eaten up alive by the fierce tailor ants. Yet it could not bring itself to admit defeat to its loud-mouthed, tiny opponent who miraculously continued to sound in top form. Finally Obu died off in the effort at a last incoherent and inaudible reply.

Nza called, and there was no response. It called again, and again in cheerier and cheerier tones but there was no longer any response from *Obu*. *Nza* became convinced that its dull-witted opponent had given up the contest - dead. So it flew cross to the other tree and found the bones of *Obu*, nibbled white by the tailor ants, at the foot of the tree. Without showing any pity, *Nza* picked up a femur from the heap of bones and fashioning it into a flute, blew the following victory melody:

Tutuli tuu li-li-li   Anu melu onwe ya (the poor chap killed itself).

This story offers a vocal dimension to mime only in so far as it is necessary to interpret the moods suggested by the songs in the story as mimicry.

Now let each student write down first, then relate at least one folk story involving as many characters as possible. Animal types should be represented in mime. All stories offering dramatizable features should be mimed as class exercises. If by the time you conclude the exercises you have an impressive collection of short plays in mime, it would be worthwhile staging an evening performance of mime with costumes and possibly dance for your school audience. If your performances are well received by your school audience then write for a television audition. Folk tales dramatized in mime and costume would be very much loved by not only children television viewers but by adults as well.

d. The following exercises have been selected because they should give you specific practices on acting. They will involve you in all the elements of acting: characterisation, elocution, stage movement and mood interpretation. They are short excerpts from written (not necessarily published) plays. They have been chosen because of the special problems in empathic acting. which they pose. It is recommended that the students should memorise the parts first. It is the only way that the interpretation which is expected of them will be meaningful and rewarding exercises. Where it is necessary, just enough background information on an excerpt has been given to help the actors capture the circumstances and mood of the characters before the excerpt. Representative stage setting and stage props are recommended for these exercises even if they have to be school desks and chairs.

1

Ifufe: Yes, make an offer. Another healthy white slave from the sunny state of America for sale. You must not miss him. Make your offers. This one is strong and healthy and he can guarantee you twelve hours of hard work without food. All he needs is just a cup of water every six hours. When the water is not available you don't have to bother, he drinks his own sweat. Very economical slave-labour as long as you gag him to prevent his expending his abundant energy talking. His language is explosive but that is no problem if your whip is handy. He is an insurance against bankruptcy. He is a prize slave who can double the average slave output and double your revenue. A most valuable investment to own him. Look at his muscles. He is very serious looking, serious minded but equally very obedient and tireless as long as he constantly hears the song of a whip. Now come on, you prosperous property owners, be the lucky owner. Make an offer for this indispensable slave ... Yes ... one bag of cowries? No, no no ... not for this one. Take another look at him ... what do you say? ... oh come on, that's a paltry sum for such a useful commodity, such a sturdy beast of burden. Come on, shake your money bags and your money safes. Your money ain't no use if it is being locked up without being doubled. And here is a wonder money doubler I assure you. I wouldn't part with him for five bags ... what say you? This slave can easily earn you the five bags you invest on him in under a week of supervised slave-labour. Never mind his complexion. It is not caused by sickness, definitely not the white-skin-disease. It is to show off his veins and help you assess when he is exerting his maximum muscle power. Mind you he is equally at his best when the sun is hottest as when the rain is stormiest. ...he is not even mildly interested in brooding over the lack of female company which is such a problem with most slaves nowadays... Come on you landowners, better offers...

(The Timeless Woman materialises)

T.W.: Five and half bags of cowries and I hope he is worth it.

Lfufe: Hear! hear! Five and half bags from the beautiful and enchanting lady. Never mind madam, he is worth every cowry piece you invest in him. He promises you that or your money back. Any more attractive offers? Do you want my lady to be the lucky possessor of this prize specimen of a slave ...? Well ... going ... going ... A deal!

Congratulations, my lady. No problem at all with him. A perfect lamb when you show him the anger of a whip. He is a jackass when it comes to serviceability. A perfect money's worth of donkey labour.[4]

The above monologue is a vocal banter. The actor must possess a cheerful, boisterous personality, in fact he should be a talkative comedian. An auctioneer's style of elocution is needed. Note that later in the bargaining, the auctioneer starts a one-sided dialogue with the audience. Passages like this require special skill as a persuasive speaker. You either sweep the audience off their feet with the severity of your humour during the harangue or you bore them with your colourlessness. Since you are delivering severe humour, you must keep a straight face, any smile or grin you show must be to encourage your audience, not in appreciation of yourself.

For effective dramatization provide the slave with a rope around his neck. Ifufe should hold the free end of the leash. He should also carry a whip which is recommended in the dialogue. A good actor should involve the slave in the action. For instance at "... if your whip is handy" the whip should be cracked on the floor by the side of the slave who should react appropriately to show fear (of further public degradation). That apart, the resentment of the slave should be made manifest all through, matching the insults by Ifufe. At "... Look at his muscles "...pinch the slave's muscles and make him wince. Use the whip occasionally but effectively to make the slave cower - more especially if you notice his resentment is becoming pronounced - that would humiliate him. As with story-telling sessions, in plays make sure you engage the audience as if they are your customers.

Although referred to as a monologue, note that the stage activity involves more than one actor - in fact three visible actors.

---

[4] Meki Zewi: The Tree Woman Series: From Episode ill, "Tree Woman vs Slavery.

* * *

2

Dr. Ita has been ordered by Mr. Dagbeni to kill Uloma in order to suppress a top society scandal threatening both of them by Uloma's continued existence. Dr. Ita is not naturally a killer. Moreover, the ethics of the medical profession forbid him killing a patient. But Mr. Dagbeni is posing a more terrifying threat should the doctor fail to carry out the murder. Uloma is unaware of any danger to her life, least of all from Dr. Ita who is both her doctor and a friend. Now Dr. Ita has brought Uloma to his clinic to administer the deadly injection recommended by Mr. Dagbeni.

Uloma: Every night, when he came to see me, he would be trembling as you are now, every time I stroked his hair.

It was ever so funny, but he was kind to me. He only asked me to stroke his hair for him, and as soon as I started, he would start trembling and breathing fast until he started to moan.

Then he would relax, full of sweat, and thank me.

At first I was frightened.

But he told me it is a game he enjoys playing.

Very funny man.

He never tried to make physical love to me the way you flied.

And he always brought such magnificent presents every time he came

You are not even Listening to me, hid

(Dr. Ita, who has been fidgeting with a syringe, whirls round looking wild and panicky)

Doctor: Yes.

Uloma: You are very sick.

Doctor: I am not sick.

Uloma: You are.

You are trembling

Is it cold?

Doctor. I am not!

It is not.

(Uloma stands, moves closer)

Uloma: Do you want me to stroke your hair?

(Doctor backs away upstage, scared)

(She raises her hand)

Doctor: No!

Please don't!

Uioma: Well, what's the matter with you?

(Uloma resumes her seat)

Whenever I stroked John, he used to recover after some time.

Doctor. I am not John.

Uloma: Who said you are?

I only wanted to tranquilise you.

Doctor: *(ruminatively)* Tranquilise – Tranquiliser

Don't use that word again!

Uloma: What is wrong with the word?

Why are you so agitated?)

Are you remembering a very bad dream?

Doctor: No! - Yes - a bad dream - tranquiliser - tranquiliser - which one is the reliable tranquiliser?

(He turns and moves back to the table)

Uloma: You are saying the same word.

Doctor: What word?

Now, come on and take your tranquiliser.

(With resolution, he tries to steady his hand and operate the syringe)

Uloma: Well, I've been waiting...[5]

*   *   *

---

[5] From Meki Zewi: "A Drop of Honey".

When you are afraid or morally weak about a situation you are bound to show visible give-away signs of your state of mind.

Dr. Ita has got his unsuspecting victim ready, yet he is finding it difficult to select and prepare the appropriate deadly injection (euphemistically called "a tranquiliser" by the man who ordered the killing.) In his agitation Dr. ha shows that he has been sapped of the necessary moral or physical strength to carry out the act. Uloma still sees him as a harmless friend. Dr. Ita's state of nerves should be registered for the benefit of the audience while Uloma is taking her first lines. Watch out for other significant clues to your stage activities which are contained in the dialogue.

3

(Nene is so absorbed in staring at Panda that she is unaware of the man who, evidently tipsy, is fervently asking for her attention)

Man: Shay gir-r-rl, you look a sweet, oop-ah-h-mean-e-em-coot. 11mm-a shentlemanish-shit-hurnph-diSh huh? C'mon-give ush a look huh? *(he sings ad lib)*
Your eyesh are bright Your lipsh are full
Your cheeksh-
(He attempts to caress her cheek)

Nene: (startled) WHAT!!
(Man jumps back nearly toppling over, shrugs and staggers away uncaring.[6]

*   *   *

What is important here is the drawling and sloppy speech that characterises a drunk, the hiccups and the inability to coordinate one's faculties which leads to unsteady deportment (whether stationary or moving). This is one of those rare instances where an actor is expected to exhibit weak deportment on stage.

Think about a drunk. He feels like a ship being heavily rocked about by turbulent waves. For him the earth and all in

---

[6] From Meki Zewi'"' Lazy Boncs"

it become a slowly revolving mass rocking him off balance. His general weakness of form must be reflected starting from the droop of his pendulating head to the unsteadiness of his stance and to the lurch with which he attempts the caress.

4

Chief Ekpelinia: Now you loveliest of the lovelies
What is keeping you back?
Come, fly into my noble embrace and feel my overpowering need for you
(The Timeless Woman does not move. Chief Ekpelima Moves closer to her, puzzled. He attempts to grab her, but the Timeless Woman holds up one hand and he stops)

Timeless Woman: Don't touch me - yet.

Chief Ekpelima: *(Explodes and stampedes up and down with fury)*
What! What!! Don't touch you! No! No!!
No living earthling has ever dared say that to Chief Otaka Ekpelima. No woman of flesh and blood has ever dreamed it. They have always thanked me for condescending to give them pleasure. No woman! No! Never! .*(He turns towards her)*
Not even you with all the glories of your face and form would dare - *(Change of voice, with puzzlement)*
What are you smiling at? You look so delicious when you add a smile to that face.
Now my queen, my idol, my ideal, don't play so difficult to get. Come on, fly into your lord's embrace.

(He begins to move in again. The Timeless Woman holds up her hand and points to the direction of Ifufe)

Timeless Woman: My brother is watching.

Chief: How dares he!
                    Your brother? Ah yes, your brother.
                    Well, what is he doing here anyway?
                    Why didn't he vamoose with the rest of
his kind?
                    (He hollers at Ifufe) Eh, You!
                    Why didn't you clear out with the rest?
                    (He advances bullyingly at Ifufe)
                    Come on, be gone! Outside! Away with
                    you! You can come back and collect her
                    when I am satisfied No! Oh No. You
                    don't come back. She now has the
                    honour and singular privilege of being my
                    own. She will now be mine, permanently.
                    Now, away with you! Away!

Timeless Woman: *(protesting)* He is my brother.

Chief: *(brusquely)* So what?

Timeless Woman: *(with authority)* Nobody howls at my
                    brother.

Chief: *(amazed)* Did I hear you say I howled?

Timeless Woman: Yes. You are a howling brute. Nobody
                    howls at my brother. And what is more,
                    nobody shouts in my presence!

Chief: Your presence? You dare talk to me like
                    that?

Timeless Woman: I dare talk to whom I wish anyhow I
                    like.
                    Most of all, you.

Chief: *(storms around)* Impossible! Unbearable!
                    What arrogance! Impudence! I have not
                    heard it. I will not hear it. I have been

challenged. My words, my wishes have
been challenged. I have been challenged!
By a woman. Impossible! By a woman?
Incredible! It has not happened! It did
not happen...
(to the Timeless Woman) Hei! You may be
the most beautiful angel in the firmament
and the most gorgeous queen on earth,
but you will not challenge me. Never!
Never!! (storms around)
Disrespect! Traditional abomination!
Treason!! *(calmly to T.W.)*
But, for your beauty I forgive you. Now,
your brother goes immediately or I'll
have to ignore his presence.[7]

*   *   *

This is a confrontation of personalities. A ruler who is not
used to even the slightest form of opposition to his wish or
command suddenly finds himself not only being resisted by a
'mere' woman, but even being talked down upon and ordered
about by her. Imagine his rage (his internal struggle) his
intolerance of opposition conflicting with his moral weakness
(his consuming lust for her) and both coupled to his
impotence in asserting himself before a strange woman.

What about the Timeless Woman's ease born of self
confidence and her unperturbability.

*   *   *

5

Ifufe: Shut up, you jabbering bastardly knave. How
           dare you! Alright, you will now go and kneel

---

[7] Meki Zewi: The Tree Woman Series. From Episode I "The Tree Woman vs
Ekpelima".

down over there balancing that bowl on your head without holding it.

(Logan pitifully goes to the indicated spot and to the right of Ifufe. He kneels and balances the bowl on his head)

If the bowl falls down before (1) release you, then (1) will know you did it deliberately to insult me. And of course you will be lynched or burnt publicly in the market place. But if it does not fall down before 1 am disposed to release you, then it would mean that you did it in a moment of stupid, unpardonable forgetfulness, in which case you will receive a mild chastisement of forty-eight strokes of the cane on your bare white skin, after which you will be put to task on the farms tilling with bare body for a good twelve hours non stop with neither water nor food.

Ifufe: And you *(to Bankrupt)* don't stand there assaulting (my) sight, you idiot. Run along and get a fan. Can't you see master is sweating?

(Bankrupt carefully puts down his own bowl of water and rushes into the hut to come out again with a fan. He immediately proceeds to fan Ifufe with both hands while Jfufe continues with his meal)

Ifufe: You brainless numbskull. Do you expect me to descend to your level and degrade myself by lifting the bowl of water from the ground with my superior hands? *(Bankrupt stops fanning, puts down the fan and stoops to carry the bowl of water. But Jfufe kicks his head and Bankrupt slumps on his buttocks)*

Ifufe: You blinking ass, why did you stop fanning? Simply because you have to lift the bowl of water?

(Bankrupt quickly struggles up to his feet. He picks the fan and resumes the fanning exercise with his left hand at the same time as he tries to lift the bowl of water with his

*right hand. Because he was looking at the bowl instead of
at the movement and direction of the fan, the fan hits
!fufe"'s knee and !fufe shouts at him)*

Ifufe: What! You bastard slave! You hit me!

*(Bankrupt is so nervous and startled that the bowl falls
off his hand and breaks, spattering water all over. The
shock of such a catastrophe startles Logan who shivers
and exclaims,):*

Logan: Incredible!

*(The bowl on his head trembles, unbalances, falls and
breaks)[8]*

*   *   *

1. This excerpt emphasizes the stupid foolery that arises from
   too much dread of a pain-in-the-neck termagant. There
   could be the temptation for the *actor* doing Bankrupt to
   descend to clowning. That must be checked. Clowning is a
   poor substitute for comic acting.
2. Lfufe should put into his voice such despising qualities
   that would sap a lowly personality of any human valour.
3. Logan's face and attitude where he is kneeling and carrying
   a bowl should reflect the horrors of Bankrupt's
   degradation. But he should keep a weary eye on Ifufe for
   Ifufe would obviously flay him if he is caught exhibiting
   anything but approval for Bankrupt's degradation.

*   *   *

6

Sergeant Dan is a soldier on sick leave. He has a shrapnel
injury on his right leg so he uses the aid of a walking stick. He
received the injury while trying to save one of his soldiers,
John Oko, who was the bravest boy in his platoon and a true

---

[8] Meki Zewi: The Tree Woman Series. From Episode III 'The Tree Woman vs
Slavery."

Christian who always led the platoon in prayers before battles. John died of injuries from enemy mortar bomb while Sergeant Dan was carrying him to a treatment depot. Dan has been bitter with God ever since John died in brave action. He could not understand why it was John who had to die. His meeting with Madam Oko, John's widowed mother is accidental. Madam Oko is old, very old, and supports her frail body on a crutch. An old convert to Christianity, she had become a staunch Christian.

*   *   *

1. Dab: I do not quite agree with you. I mean, what you said about His being a true and just God who will not allow His own to perish. I have seen unnecessary deaths, ma'am.

2. Madam Oko: But we speak the same language, son. But for the Lord who presided over, and stopped the killings, where shall we be now? Oh! This is indeed a sad Christmas for all Christian homes. But my Lord is awake in His heaven.

3. Dan: So you then know bitterness too?

4. Madam Oko: Bitterness! Bitterness! *(Sighs)* But the Lord is my strength and shield. God, I do not complain. Far be it from me to question your handiwork. But it is true that my only son, the only child of my womb at an age I did not know I would ever experience the joy of childbirth again - *(sighs ... a subdued trembling voice):* My child will never see Christmas again. *(supplicatingly)* God, thou giveth; thou taketh away; Glory be to thy holy name ... *(to Dan)* Son, my only boy, the joy of my heart, my dear John died six months ago in the battlefront.

(She collapses with sobs into Dan's hands. Dan supports her heaving shoulders with his free left hand)

5. Dan: Accept my sympathy ma'am. But, pardon my impertinence. Which John are you talking about? Who are You?

6. Madam Oko: *(Looking up with dry sad eyes and with surprise too)* I am Madam Oko of Ota Village.

7. Dan: (nonplussed and stuttering) Surely, you are not the mother of the late Corporal John Oko?

8. Madam Oko: That I am, son...

9. Dan: Come, come with me. There is a public square over there. Here, let me help you...
Yes, let us go and sit down ma'am.
(As they move)
We have a common grief, but
I think I have a lot to learn from you.[9]

              *   *   *

1. Madam Oko did not say anything personal in dialogue 2. It is her deep rooted grief which was portrayed in her voice in her last two statements which moved Dan to ask his question in dial 3.

2. The upsurge of grief with which she calls "Bitterness!" is purged in the sigh that follows, for unlike Dan, her own bitterness is not towards God, not towards mankind, but towards the idea of war.

3. Study carefully the implication of each line of dialogue. The way you use your voice to act the various dialogues (2 and 4) should bring out the various emotions the

---

[9] From Meki Zew,: 'Sad Christmas"

characters are going through. Study carefully the stage directions.

*   *   *

7

Dan:	*(to Madam Oko)* well, let me not delay you further. will not want you to miss the carol service altogether.

(Madam Oko, still very elated, stands up with her clutch and in her shaky old voice merrily begins to sing "God bless you Merry Gentlemen". As she sings Dan is moved more and more, until beaming with happiness he also stands up, and throwing his left hand over Madam Oko's shoulder, he joins in the singing with a robust voice.-
Suddenly Madam Oko's heart fails. She chokes and coughs, and is saved from falling, as she loses grip of her crutch, by Dan who bears her weight. Her eyes roll in agony and begin to glaze over as her life ebbs away. Dan takes her to a comfortable sofa and holds her racking body)

Madam Oko: *(Brokenly)* Son, my hour is come. The dizziness is on me. My spirit is strong, but this old body has been weakened by the deprivation and sufferings of this unholy war.

Dan: *(all flustered and confused)* Take heart ma'am. Take it easy, and let me get you some water to drink.

Madam Oko: *(still shaking but restraining him with a fluttering shaky hand)*
No son, it is too late. This flesh is now too weak for my spirit. The Lord calls on me.

Dan: *(alarmed as it dawns on him that she is dying, he supports her from behind the chair)*

Don't say that ma'am. Hero, let me help you.

Madam Oko: *(sinking some more into the chair in spites of his support, and her eyes rolling with unearthly fire as the whites begin to show, she speaks brokenly still)* No son, God has done His work by me, and now calls me to him. This flesh must now rest forever. Oh -what a sad christmas. Yet my spirit goeth forth with joy. *(Her head rolls back, but she struggles back to life)* Sing the carols son, sing, sing, sing. *(Dan burst into a sad rendition of "Hark the Herald Angels Singing". As he sings, his apprehension is clearly written on his face and the alarm with which he looks at Madam Oko whose features are calmed by the song, eyes closed, while the rest of her body is being racked occasionally with the struggles of her departing breath. Dan's voice tails off...)*

Madam Oko: Here, hold my hand. *(Dan 4f1s the indicated hand)* Promise me you will not grieve again.

Dan: I promise you Mother

Madam Oko: Yes, the carols must go on. I can already hear the angels singing *(Her eyes open and begin to roll up the white as death throbs seize her body again)* ... Sing on son. Sing on... S-I-N-G On and ... speed ... my ... spirit ... to ... my ... God. *(with that she jerks up convulsively and dies. Dan who is now bearing her dead weight, gently lays her body on the chair with sad slow and mournful demeanor. He takes a long sorrowful look at the reposed body of Madam Oko. Then he shakes his*

head, picks up his fallen walking stick, and with a
parting look he takes his exit much shaken)[10]

*   *   *

1.   Generally, scenes that should arouse pathetic emotions are more difficult to act than most other types. The audience prefers outright violence which gives them some thrill to a pathetic scene that involves them in emotional empathy. Any opportunity given the audience by the actors to abnegate emotional empathy through laughter is quickly grabbed by members of the audience to convince themselves that it is not real life. If a very sad or pitious scene is taking place on stage, and gives the audience cause for superficial thrill or amusement, then the action on stage is an acting failure.

2.   Our audiences have been known to laugh when death or misfortune occurs on stage. This is because most actors make dying on stage a clownish process. Death scenes, especially the type that occur in this excerpt should be acted with pathos. There should be nobility in it. Well done, the audience, no matter how sadistic or remote, no matter how much they think of the dying as a mere stage pretence, cannot fail to be deeply moved, although with a tinge of gratefulness: that the dear old soul died happily and contentedly. The author has seen members of the audience weep at Madam Oko's death during performances of this play.

3.   Ordinarily Dan as a soldier who has seen action in the battlefield should not be unduly shaken by deaths. But he is deeply moved by Madam Oko's death because within a very few hours of their meeting, she had performed a miracle on him (for which he started calling her "Mother"): She healed his spiritual wounds. What is more, her son, John, who was equally dear to Dan, died in Dan's arms while Dan was carrying him out of the battlefield. It was a

---

[10] From Meki Zewi: "Sad Christmas"

death that made Dan break faith with God as a true and just God: Such true human beings like John shouldn't die so young and without justification even if they are soldiers. And now here is the mother, a noble woman dying in his arms too

4. Dan's exit is important. In his drooping shoulders, his harassed facial features, his pain-dulled eyes, his general tiredness of deportment which makes him lean too heavily on his walking stick as he limps off stage, the audience should glimpse his state of mind.

*　　*　　*

8

1. Nene: Don't be impossible my dear.
2. Dede: Of course not. *(sinks more comfortably into his chair)* Thunderface will not touch me with a sterilised or insulated pole and you know it.
3. Nene: *(coming over to hand him a glass of beer and kneeling by his side).* Well, he has invited us to join his group, and it is our big chance.
4. Dale: Leavemeoutofit.
5. Nene: *(hurt)* I can't leave you out of it. I did it for YOU.
6. Dede: Look, have you gone ga-ga? Or what are you talking about?
7. Nene: *(sighing, she explains patiently)* Dede—it is like this. Ego took me to the party; a party thrown by Pongo Panda. And by the way. Willy has been signed on too by Panda.
8. Dale: You don't mean it.
9. Nene: But I do. And he is to be featured in the coming Show Biz Festival
10. Dede: Well, roast me for an over-sized snail.
11. Nene: *(Hopefully)* Of course you'll be roasted. So darling,) during the party, I got Thunderface interested in us. *(The warmth leaves his face and he*

loses interest once again and concentrates on his beer.
Nene becomes agitated and anxious, pleading).

12. Nene   Please Dede, you must accept. It is our big chance. You must! You MUST!!

13. Dale: All right my dear, relax. Just what do I do to measure up to Panda's standards? Tell me.

14. Nene: *(earnestly)* You already have a good tone on your instrument. All that is required of you now is hard-work. Take lessons in the morning; practice on your own in the evenings; and still play at the joint at night. I will be doing the same thing too. No doubt in a week's time, when he expects us to appear at the season's auditions for the festival, we will be in top form.

15. Dede: Top form indeed. I will work hard. Oh yes! Lessons in the mornings; practices in the evenings and performances at nights. All by me. Great!! You have it all neatly worked out. Sorry to disappoint you. I have no intention of going into all the labour for your wild goose chase. You cannot kid Thunderface Panda. Nobody ever does.

16. Nene: *(desperate, she nags)* It is not a wild goose chase! You must get rid of the complex worrying you. And the only way is to work hard. But you are just lazy, lazy, lazy! You cannot help yourself and you will not allow anybody else to help you. You sit down there satisfied with third rate standards when you can do better. An opportunity to prove and improve yourself comes, and you won't be bothered at all. Stick in the mud! Sit in that lazy chair from morning till night, just dozing and smoking and—

17. Dale: *(exploding and jumping)* All right!! Now stop it!! Stop nagging me!

18. Nene: I will not stop unless you promise to do something for yourself.

19. Deck: *(shouting and gesticulating)* In that case, get out of here. Get out of my room! You are not my wife, and it is not your damn business what I do with myself.

20. Nene: *(shocked and shattered)* Oh.... *(she turns away)*

21. Dale: *(still shouting at her)* Yes! And I will not have you or any other of your type disturb my peace, or order me about. If I am lazy, it is none of your business, you hear? Now get out! Get out of here before I throw you I out I don't want anything more to do with you or your Thunderface. *(Nene weakly collapses on the bed and looks up to him pitifully)*

22. Nene: Oh Dede, You can't be saying all that to me —

23. Dale: Oh yes I can. And I am!

24. Nene: *(reduced to tears)* Darling, have a heart. It is not fair. I was doing it all for you.[11]

*　　　*　　　*

1. Dede is a lazy cynic. Nene is a bustling go-getter. Nene starts her lines full of excitement. In dialogue 12 Nene speaks with a tone of rising emphasis. Dialogue 14 says "earnestly." So she should increase the tempo of her speech and enthusiasm. When you are persuading somebody to see your point of view your rate and heat of communication normally rises. In dialogue 16, her tone becomes desperate and, therefore, should suggest some irritation. Her voice starts getting shrill. She could try standing up on the first line of dialogue 16 and stamping her foot with rising heat to emphasize "lazy, lazy, lazy." Then pause for five seconds glaring at him furiously before the next line. Make "stick in the mud" sharp like a slap because that is the line that finally galvanises Dede into the

---

[11] From Mekj Zewi: "Lazy Bones"

offensive. Pause for a count of three seconds then start the last line at the top of your voice with a touch of hysteria.

Dede's shouting should be so unexpected and powerful that it shuts off Nene's outburst and leaves her gaping. Dialogue 18 is a desperate attempt by Nene to assert her stronger character. She is shocked and shattered in dialogue 20 because, although it is not an issue in their love, marriage has been taken for granted in their relationship. Her tone in dialogue 22 is an appeal to Dede to be reasonable, probing for a reassurance from him of his love. She could bat her eyelids a couple of times in an unsuccessful attempt to hold back the tears that should prepare us for the stage direction in dialogue 24. Her resolve and strength break when he says dialogue 23. The tears should be seen before dialogue 24 which should be said in a weeping voice, not necessarily with sobs. Crying and weeping do not mean covering and rubbing your eyes with your hands and making some funny insincere sounds as most poor amateurs do. The pathos is more when the audience sees tear-brimmed eyelids or tear drops descending down your sad cheeks. Nene did not voluntarily want to cry. Crying here is an inevitable emotional outlet for the magnitude of the hurt she is feeling. She should feel the tear drops on her lap or hands before she even realises she is crying and then attempts to wipe the tears with whatever is handy. If the part is acted with the empathy it deserves, i.e., if you do it as if it is happening to you in real life, you shouldn't even need the stage direction to dialogue 24 to make you weep. Well acted, you could excite sympathetic tears in the audience who witnessed your devotion to your man as well as your sincere selfless efforts to help your lover being so brutally rewarded.

Dede as a cynic is stubborn about his own assessment of issues and people. Nenes enthusiasm is wasted on him. He is self-satisfied though not necessarily progressive. His voice remains on an indifferent level giving the impression that his replies are merely to humour Nene. But at dialogue *15,* he begins to show impatience. If he were lounging in the chair he should sit up. But he could resume his relaxed apathy after his last line which should be given in a tone that says "Now let's drop the topic."

Dialogue 17 says "exploding and jumping." It is one fast continuous movement that takes him from his reclining position to an aggressive standing position, facing and domineering over Nene.

This means that Nene should have been standing well away from the chair to the left or right of Dede who was sitting facing the audience. Moving away from the chair will give them room for action with no awkwardness such as knocking against a chair. Note in the stage blocking that Nene's standing position before Dede jumps up must be between Dede's chair and the bed or couch. She turns away and moves towards the bed/couch with no undramatic necessity to by-pass Dede or the chair. Dede would lose strength following Nene. He should take dialogue 21 with determination, standing where he first confronted her. He stays there for dialogue 23. We are not told what happens after dialogue 24. If Dede relents, he will show it not necessarily in his next words but in the way he moves across to Nene. If he is the hard-hearted type he might turn round and resume his seat and drink.

*　　　　*　　　　*

9

A bully is usually a person who suffers from a complex and therefore tries to use his/her advantages of size or position to intimidate those whom he/she is afraid of. This exercise is a difficult scene from a tragedy. It calls for experience and talent for an effective portrayal. As a study in powerful personality clash between a man and a woman each of whom is torn by a

mental conflict of two strong forces: moral duty and emotional
love, it also constitutes a deep study in self-torment.

Urora is a war captive while Waspi is the field commander
whose forces captured Urora.

*   *   *

*(Waspi looks at Urora standing by his side and his fury calms down
to tenderness and love. He goes to Urora, holds her fondly as he
says—)*

1. Waspi: Sorry love, I was carried away. Mind not my
   outburst. *(But Urora is deeply hurt. She brushes off his
   hold and runs out of his embrace declaiming—)*

2. Urora But they come from your heart! *(This taunt
   maddens Waspi who jumps at her with—)*

3. Waspi: Woman! *(He checks himself. Looks with surprise at his
   wide spread fingers that nearly encircled her throat. He
   checks himself, but the fury and madness are still in him
   as he side steps with a fierce warning-)* Taunt me not
   with my weakness. For though your people are
   not born slaves, yet have I the power to make
   you my slave.

   (Urora braces up with provoked pride, and announces spiritedly—)

4. Urom: A Singhali woman slaves for no one. Rather
   death from the hands of a puppet than slavery at
   the court of a king. *(Waspi winces with pain but
   immediately undergoes a somersault if emotions. He
   laughs wildly and harshly as he appraises the challenge in
   her eyes).*

5. Waspi: You Singhalese *have* wonderful courage, and
   deserve the admiration of the gods (steps away
   d.s.) Most kings are just fortunate cowards with
   lesser cowards to obey their commands. The
   Tribains are the fortunate cowards. And we
   Rhankrajis the lesser cowards. No wonder we
   have conspired and combined, to crush your
   courage and superiority. *(He strides R.S. front,
   weakly and humbly. With his eyes staring longingly to the*

skies he intones the following wish—) Yet, before I die,
ye gods, may it be my privilege to win the love of
this Singhali woman, that my future generations
will boast kinship with such a free and proud
race— *(With the same humility and tiredness he goes
over to Urora and once more pledges his love).* Urora, I
will *cherish* and honour you, if you will accept my
love and be my wife *(then with a touch of boas(ful
pride)* To share in the glory of my conquests. *(Once
again Urora recoils from his touch, her eyes still blazing
her challenge and defiance as she rages—)*

6. Urora: Conquests! Conquests, you shameless warrior?
Has it never occurred to you, that a conqueror
can still be the slave of the vanquished? As the
gods have so decreed, Singhali is not a slave race.
Any impostors who sit on her throne, will still be
the slaves of those they pretend to rule. *(Waspi is
looking tortured. His breath comes in gasps with the
restraint with which he is absorbing her taunts. Urora
moves up close to him and with deliberation and emphasis
addresses him).*

7. Urora: My friend—
There is more honour in leaving Singhali alone,
than in attempting to conquer her. Military
conquests you may temporarily achieve, but the
will of the people is indomitable. *(Then fiercely she
admonishes him with a final outburst).* Go! Tell your
masters, convince them, that in Singhali,
conquest will forever elude you! *(Waspi lunges
again for her throat with his two hands as he shouts).*

8. Waspi: WOMAN! *(Urora leaps out of his reach. His hands
trembling with the cauldron of emotions boiling inside him,
Waspi draws away in shame, staring wildly and
unbelievingly at his outspread fingers—)* The more you
taunt me, the more I love you *(Waspi moves over to
his table R.S. and leans weakly on it).* Oh, my heart is

bitter for the carnage I have wrought, and the destruction I still have to execute. *(He walks back to Urora, takes her gently by the shoulder and starts moving slowly to C.S.)*

Come, keep me company for the night. Or else, the ghosts of the innocent civilians, slaughtered by my men at my order, will torment me yet another night. *(He leaves her CS. and Urora drifts back to L.S. front. Waspi declares with feeling—)* How I dread these nightmares. Rather, a misprisionist bullet through my heart. Yet, I choose to live and suffer nightmares; for slaves are despicable cowards. *(He stands forlornly. Urora looks at him with pity and slowly drifts to him as she says—)*

9. Urora: I have admiration for you as a man, but contempt for what you represent. *(Then she pleads with him desperately)*

Your captive though I am, to spare or spoil as you please, yet I implore you, for the love you've professed, leave me alone. *(She steps away from him giving vent to her emotions as they possess her)* You Rhankrajis have remorselessly wounded us for over two years now; it will be defilement for me to give what you want. The ghosts of my slaughtered relations will torment me all my life. *(She turns and challenges Waspi who has once again started heaving with suppressed violence as her words mock and thrash him).* You've driven a dagger through my heart yet you speak to me of love. Oh no, Singhalese are your masters, a master does not marry a slave.

But you are a true slave. Do yourself one original service for which I will, even in death, cherish your love. Kill me without torturing me, or else set me free to go back to my people. *(She steps away from him in torment).* I wish I could love you, for you are better than your fellows. *(Suddenly she seems possessed).*

But it will be a betrayal of my people's sufferings. No.

Blood is thicker than water *(and very proudly she declaims).* Dead or alive, Singhali will not suffer disgrace through me. *(Waspi's restraint breaks at that and his temporary madness becomes violent. He flies at Urora's throat with his two hands. This time, he is squeezing the life out of her as he wildly yells—)*

10. Waspi: You temptress! You torturer! *(Urora who is ineffectively fighting to free her throat cries out in a strangulated voice)*

11. Urora You hurt me! *(Her cry jolts Waspi into consciousness of his action, and he immediately releases her and steps out but the rage and madness are still very much in him as he raves—)*

12. Waspi: Everything have I offered you, and insults have I got in return. Yet will I not kill you. You have too much courage for me to turn you loose to my men to defile as they have defiled a few of your stupid country girls who could not recognise that they are superior to those to whom they expose their womanhood. You are a credit to your people; but you are a distractor. *(He braces up militarily).* A true soldier has no place for emotions and sentiments. *(He swivels suddenly and poses like a stalking panther, demented, his eyes staring murder, his features shockingly frightful. Then with slow deliberate intent he begins to stalk Urora, who as if hypnotised is staring impotently with horror, her mouth open but bringing out no sound. Waspi's voice is grating, dangerously subdued—~* I hate you as much as I love you. *(Now close to her, he grabs her. Pinioning her two hands to her body, he fiercely turns round with her and begins to advance slowly R.S. keeping her in front, his red unblinking*

tormented eyes boring through her. Her feeble attempts at resistance are lost on Waspi's firm deadly grasp—). Shall I kill you with my hands? Or, let you go back to your people? Which will you call weakness—To kill you or to set you free? *(Then he shakes her violently)* Tell me; Tell me! Tell me! *(he roars).* Tell me my love, my hate!! Which is more honourable— To kill you, or to set you free? Tell me you Singhali woman. *(He has now taken her D.SR.*

His torment is contorting his facial features-) I see— You will not tell me. *(with venom)* You wretch! *(with that he flings her down violently. He stares at her).* You despise me. *(He steps away towards C.S.)* No! It is not me. It is my slavish weakness that you despise. *(Now C.S. He tears at his hair and goes berserk as he yells)* You make me mad! *(Urora has got up. Waspi turns on her again breathing murder. Urora dodges back until the R.S. wall stops her. She is very much frightened)* I wish I could kill you— Yes, kill you and plant my gene in you. *(He has come close to her and with a strangulated cry, Urora swoons and collapses on the ground)* But then, dead, you cannot bear my child. *(He tears his eyes off her and yells)* Ye gods!! I am running mad. Orderly! *(Waspi is standing C.S. hands akimbo, breathing heavily and does not look Urora's way again. Orderly runs in and salutes smartly. Waspi barks out—).* Take her away! Let nobody touch or soil her! Leave her free to go where she wills—It is an order! *(He bears down on a surprised Orderly jabbing a pointed finger at him as he threatens—)* I will shoot any dirty villain that dares look at her. *(Back to his position C.S.)* Woman! If I ever see you again, I will crush what you represent and that will mean crushing you. Take her out of my sight! *(Orderly goes over to carry Urora out).*[12]

1. You are advised to read through the passage a couple of times in order to understand Urora's personality, and Waspi's passion and desperation not only to win her love but to subdue her will power and its socio-political source of strength. If you cannot empatically feel the emotions aroused by each line of the dialogue, you cannot carry the parts. Most of the emotions implied in the lines must be apparent in your voice. And there are constant changes of emotion from one sentence to another. The characters are experiencing varied but strong emotional turmoils from beginning to end of the scene. Note that, and go through the excerpt with mounting pathos and dignity. There is more danger of under-acting than of over-acting in a scene of this emotional intensity. All movements must be meaningfully blocked and timed.

2. A few more guides that would assist you:

Waspi: In dialogue 5 change voice, and sound philosophical after line 2. Let the audience get that "admiration" in your voice in the first two lines. Then pause, but don't move. Focus your eyes at the top far corner wall of the hall, and in a philosophical voice take lines 2 to 7. Obey the stage directions as given and take lines 8-11 in a supplicatory voice. When you move up to Urora, stand abreast of her and hug her shoulders endearingly with one hand. Your voice for lines 12-15 should be rich and tender coming from your soul. Then take line 14 as directed.

Dialogue 8, lines 1 to 4 should be said in a harsh, desperate voice. But mellow down and show some tender feelings by line 6. Put a lot of feeling into lines 10-13.

Dialogue 12: Stand still, feet slightly apart in a military attitude and exude strength. Turn your face away from her for line 6. After line 27, pause and stand still for lines 20-2 1 and

---

[12] From Meki Zewi's "Urora"

obey the stage direction. Move again after line 29. You will be in position and at a standstill for lines 23 to 28.

Urora: Dialogue 6: First line is an angry outburst. Keep the emotion in your voice all through.

Dialogue 7: Put a lot of pity in the first line and let it hang for a few counts while you mentally remind yourself of your duty to your beleaguered suffering relations. Then get emphatic from line 2. You should loose sympathy for his personal feelings towards you and the war by line 6. Give line 6 with admonishing arrogance. It could be effective to take three steps away from him after line 5, then swivel into scene to confront him. Fling out the appropriate hand as you say "Go."

Dialogue 9: Start with pity in the first line but become contemptuous by line 2. Lines 7-9 should be harsh while lines 10 and 11 should give us a feeling of the ghosts in action. Lines 12-16 have suppressed violence, while lines 17-20 are conciliatory. Let (is feel your torment in lines 21 and 22. By line 26 your tone is convincingly uncompromising.

Chapter 5

Are You Ready?

Are you now ready to "walk the boards;" whether as part of your course-work, as an amateur, or as a promising professional? Then here are the things you must be doing and thinking about. If you fail to take them seriously you will be losing your chances of ever making an impression or a name or a career on stage as an actor.

You must be punctual to rehearsals or performances. An actor who fails to "beat the call" is insulting his/her fellow actors, and what is worse, the director as well as the school authority or the organisation producing the play. On stage no one is more important than the other person whether you are playing the lead role or merely a stage hand shifting props. In school, college or amateur club productions every actor, male or female, big or small, must take part in setting up the stage, and in striking the set after a performance or rehearsal, and finally in tidying up the stage or hall. The stage manager is the foreman directing these activities, not the labourer slaving for you. One of the best arrangements that ensures speed, efficiency and team spirit is to assign specific props or specific sections of the set to specific individual(s) — actor or otherwise. Thus during time for setting up whether on tour or in your resident theatre, each member of the team must carry on stage and fix his or her "bit" of the stage set/prop in a rehearsed order. After the show he/she must dismantle and carry off stage his/her section before changing into street clothes. The activity that marks setting up and striking the stage/scene should be likened to a colony of ants building their home. If you are there on time and carry out your part, the stage will be set in no time, and dismantled before the last member of the audience leaves the hall. You will therefore be free to prepare yourself personally to go on stage; or to see friends and admirers after the show. If you default, then you will disorganise and delay the entire team. Stage setting and striking as team work should form part of rehearsal schedule for every play until the process is as perfect as the production itself. In schools or colleges marks should be lost for not fitting into the drill on any particular occasion.

If for any reason you find that you are unable to attend a rehearsal, or you have to be late, you must endeavour by all means to send prior information in good time to the director or stage manager. Do not ever think that because you are an understudy or a stage hand you are not as important as the next person and therefore can afford to be late or absent. You never know when your big chance of a lifetime will come, and so don't take chances with the little you have been given. You never can tell! And, any way, your presence, and at the stipulated time, is an encouragement and a morale booster to your colleagues.

Once performances have been fixed, you have no justification whatsoever to miss any public show. You will be risking your success in class-work, or in a career, if you fail your audience. It is never done. Your self-respect, your image as a responsible person, your future relationship with your team-mates, directors everywhere, and the audience (even when you are out of school and looking for work or perhaps, working) will be placed in jeopardy if you disappoint and thereby ignore your audience. On the other hand, we have had instances of conscientious ex-school/college actors who found employers and members of the public eager to solve their problems in every aspect of their post-school lives simply because their stage manners made favourable impressions on their audiences.

You must know your lines in time. You waste the time of the other actors, and insult your directors when, during rehearsals, you are found to be stumbling over your lines and cues; or worse still to be handling your script at a time you should be concentrating on your stage presence and stage movements. A conscientious actor starts going on stage from the first day of rehearsals when the director starts the stage business. If you do that, you will discover that by the first night of performance you are already living your part naturally instead of merely acting it or, worse still, fumbling through it. You easily put off your fellow actors when you are not doing your part well. You make it difficult for them to have a smooth and empathic performance. Remember that you require all your faculties for establishing your stage presence. If you know your lines in the first scene but you are not confident with your lines in the third scene, you will discover that while acting scene 1 you are preoccupied and anxious about scene III. So you end up stumbling through scene I mechanically like a robot. And by the time you came to scene III you can no longer concentrate, due to nervousness and confusion. You may only end up ruining the scene through either forgetting your lines or jumping cues, or tripping other actors. In short you will become a nuisance to others. Everything worth doing is worth doing well. If you are going on stage, then do it to the best of your ability and responsibleness. It does not matter whether it is because you love it, or you have to do it as part of your course work. The most unexpected events could have far reaching results. It never pays to take reckless chances with any aspect of your life. Your success or failure could depend on the issues you tend to treat with levity or carelessness.

During rehearsals don't be afraid to make mistakes. Do not resent corrections. Do not be scared of being laughed at. You require mistakes to consolidate the correct things. If you are touchy about corrections, you will never make it. On the other hand you must be self-confident and self-reliant. Do not just depend on other people's assessment, and don't solicit approval. Your only mentors should be your director and yourself: your personal preparation and self-confidence. It will be rudeness for you as an actor to begin to heckle or correct a fellow actor in the presence of the director. Your fellow actor is bound to resent your arrogance, and friction might develop which could make you unpopular, and might even mar the progress of the rehearsal, thereby wasting valuable time and morale. The director is the only person authorised to guide an actor. He is the specialist whose interpretation of a play or a character is final. If he makes any mistakes, he takes the responsibility. Should you for any reason have any idea on how the play or a character could be improved, go to the director privately, and humbly, offer it as a suggestion NOT as a criticism of his approach. There have been instances where actors, especially those constantly honoured with principal roles, become too conceited and indulge in openly challenging the directions of their directors, or even resent being told what to do. Such actors are silly and will be avoided by directors. This is the wrong type of temperament and could cost you your part in that or any future plays. A director does not take delight in halting you, or shouting at you, or putting you through scenes a number of times. If you do not wish to be harassed by a director, then do your homework very well. Put your entire self and ingenuity into your role.

Make notes on your script of what you are told to do and make time to try them out privately before the next rehearsal. That way you make progress. Do not depend on making casual mental notes of instructions given to you by the director, because if you forget or fail to do the required thing by the next rehearsal you will send everybody back to the previous day. Do not deceive yourself into feeling that you will perform wonders on the performance night. It is better to be over prepared for a part and be pulled down by the director than that you are ill prepared, hoping to improve as time goes on, but never making the grade by the opening night.

Finally, a cordial relationship with every member of the team makes for the best results in the best possible time. Take all the hashing from your director while on stage because he is dedicated to achieving the best interest of the production as a whole as well as your best creditable portrayal of your role. No director ever sets out to consciousntiously undermine his baby — the production, or to discourage the best possible performance from his actors. Only a demented mother sets out to deliberately murder her child. The relationship between a director and a play he/she is directing is like that between a mother and her child. If the director shouts at you or offends you outside production circumstances, you are free to react any way you deem fit. But in production circumstances he is a dictator in every sense of the word.

Never set out to steal the show. That could tempt you into over-acting. Over-acting is as discreditable as not living up to the part. When an actor tries to call unnecessary attention to himself/herself, he/she distracts the audience from what matters. Don't ever block another actor from the audience view. If you do so by accident, then ease yourself away from his/her view without making it obvious to the audience that you have blundered. On the other hand never hide behind other actors. Any time your view is blocked by a poor actor, ease into another position in style. Do not try to pull the erring actor out of your view or to caution him/her on stage.

It is weak acting to step backwards. Each time you do so you put your co-actor in a disadvantageous position for he/she would then be. tempted to talk backwards to you. At all times aim at being on a level with any actor exchanging dialogue with you. And under no circumstance should you talk towards the back of stage.

Most beginning actors think that they must give all of their lines to the protagonist whom they are supposed to be addressing. This will make the show both drab and unnatural. You do not necessarily need to be looking at, or facing a person when you are discussing with him. After all you do not stop talking because you are picking up a book or searching for something in a cupboard at a corner of a room, or behind your addressee. Your director will help you plan the distribution of your dialogue in order to make your acting natural instead of affected or stilted. As you gain experience you will need no prompting about what lines should go to the audience or to your co-actor. You can learn a lot from watching experienced actors. But never try an all out mimicry of another actor. Always bring your own authentic personality to a role.

Discipline back stage has always been a problem with our school/college/amateur groups. Discipline back stage means that you must be conscious of the fact that your set is not sound proof. When you whisper, or talk or shout or laugh, or shuffle, or commove back stage, such acts of indiscipline filter through to the audience and lower your team's reputation. Once the performance starts there should be no noise of movement or talking or laughing or quarreling back stage. Quite often the audience sees heads of actors who are back stage as they peep through the sets in an attempt to watch their colleagues who are on stage. Some even enjoy the show wildly, more than the audience without knowing that the audience is seeing their unwanted faces and expressions. It is most shameful. If you have no business back stage then stay away altogether for you could even cause obstruction to those who are legitimately supposed to be there. And anyway nobody should have any business near the stage screens or sets.

If you are preparing to move into a scene, you will profit a lot if you stay quietly at the wing and concentrate on your style of entry. Work yourself up towards the mood for your first activity on stage. That way you will make an effective entry. There was once an actor in one of our amateur groups who was inattentively bustling around back stage instead of preparing mentally and physically for his entry. Suddenly his cue came to enter a scene and his attention was even called to the fact that he was going on. He hurriedly rushed into the scene taking place on stage. But alas, he forgot why he was there! He forgot what his cue was: what his entry lines and action were supposed to be. After looking stupid for a few seconds while the actors previously on stage waited for his cue, he nervously rushed off stage to the discomfiture of his fellow actors. Of course the audience caught the joke and had a good derisive laugh at his expense and that of his embarrassed colleagues. By the time he was reminded of his entry line back stage the audience was already clapping his flabbergasted co-actors off stage.

At all times try to cooperate with your team-mates. Whether it is in the making up, or in dressing up, any help you give to a fellow actor before or during a show is a help to yourself. On stage you require the cooperation of every one to succeed. Supposing you are a haughty, uncooperative principal actor who delights in snubbing and bullying others, always expecting to be served by others. It is your cue to go on stage. And your entry line is:

Here is my locket. Take it with you. When you show it to my beloved, he will know that I sent you. He will attend to you.

Right. First of all you were late for the performance call. *You* have not bothered to cross check that your stage props including the locket are handy. And the props man could not care less, may be because you had bullied him as you arrived late for the performance. So then you move into the back stage (where your bedroom is located) on cue from a scene. You are expecting to be handed the locket as usual by the props man so that you will re-enter the scene for the above lines. But the props man is not around to hand the locket to you. And you have no idea where it could be located because you never bothered about it before that moment. To make things worse, because of your known uncooperative attitude towards your fellow team members, none of them is interested in your panic - not even to locate a substitute object for you. The unimportant props man suddenly becomes the most important person in your life. You will never go to tell the audience that it is because of the 'unknown, insignificant' backstage props man that you, their idol, ruined their theatre evening. The props man could be penahised. But your image, your reputation, will take a long time to mend. So cooperation at all levels cannot be over-stressed. You can quarrel and dislike a person outside. If two of you have to feature in the same performance, you must sink your differences and affect friendliness, and cooperate while on stage. That is part of your self-discipline. After the show you can tear each other's eyes out over your mutual grievances. For school/college group all student members of a performing team are equal and should receive equal treatment no matter what role anyone is playing in the production.

If you are now prepared, if you have now curbed your self-consciousness, if you have now relegated your self-centredness and feeling of self-importance, if you have offered and received cooperation to and from all members of your production team, then you are really poised to conquer the stage and bring the world to your feet at the footlights which will illuminate your magnificence.

In school/college drama classes, every student must keep a Drama Scrap Book [DSB]. The DSB should contain for every class production: the title and summary of a play; a write up on the author; a summary of the production business including problems, solutions, innovations, experiments and travels from the first rehearsal to the last performance; the costume/property/lighting plot; sketches of various scenic designs. The DSB should also contain the student's observations and impressions about other plays watched as well as audience attitudes during your own productions and other people's productions in which you were a member of the audience. Student's Drama Scrapbook should be inspected and graded at the end of every session by the drama teacher as part of a student's practical drama work.

Chapter 6

A Word With The Director

We feel that there is necessity to call the attention of the director and his artistic and technical team to some of the vital aspects of their responsibility which are often treated lightly:

1. Every production you embark upon must have a programme schedule. This is very important for school/college or amateur groups in which all participants including the director have various other preoccupations and/or occupations. Even in professional theatre, you must have a programme schedule because you are paying your actors for their time and talent

   On or before the first meeting with your cast, everybody must be presented with your tentative programme for the production. This programme, which should be typed and distributed, will include dates and days for rehearsals; time and places for rehearsals; those involved in each rehearsal period; tentative fixtures for dress rehearsal and performances. These details will make it possible for every artist or actor to organise himself/herself personally for rehearsals and performances. In schools, however, it is recommended that every member of the production class or team must be present during every rehearsal. Rehearsals constitute a learning process and there is always something to learn or to unlearn during every rehearsal or performance for both beginning and experienced actors and stage technicians/artists. If the director, however, wishes to hold special sessions with an actor or a group of actors in order to work out some special problems, such extra sessions should not concern others, and should be arranged privately at the convenience of the director and those concerned.

2. Casting is an important aspect of the director's preparation for a production. In schools, effort should be made to give every member of a class an opportunity to act, or to

participate actively on stage in any other capacity - designs, construction, properties, publicity, research, etc. There is a lot of practical training in leadership, self-discipline, self-discovery, co-operation, self-confidence, team spirit, responsibility, initiative, etc. to be gained from every production experience.

In schools, double casting should be encouraged. And any actor who has put in adequate enthusiasm should be given a chance to face the audience. The student may not ever again have such an opportunity, and such an experience could change a student's vision and assessment of himself/herself. This does not mean that the quality of a production has to be sacrificed in such an exercise. You must therefore take into account a student's physical qualifications for the various roles first and foremost. Then during normal class-work and exercises or separate auditions, suitability in terms of elocution and other aspects of acting should be assessed to guide you in assigning roles. Do not be afraid to encourage a reluctant potential.

Those extroverts clamouring for roles may not necessarily be the best actors in the roles they lobby for. A competent director should have the intuitive acumen that senses hidden potential which needs to be exposed.

Prepare a comprehensive actors' list which should contain the assets and liabilities of every student against his/her name. Not only will this be a form of progress chart from which you can assess and grade each student in practical theatre, it would also be a reference record for your casting and recommendation exercises.

3. With the help of your stage manager and designers, prepare the property plot, the costume plot, and the various designs for the technical aspects of the production in time. Ensure that each team is working hard. The sooner your actors can rehearse within the set and with the right properties, the easier your task of directing, and the faster they can relax in their roles. You must avoid rushing everything and everybody at the last moment; or planting your actors on the day of performance in a set strange to

them and/or with props they've never tried out before. It would be like transplanting a groomed palm tree to a strange garden and expecting it to yield immediately without getting used to the new soil.

You must above all never give the impression to any member of your team or class that he/she is unwanted or useless. Every member of the team or class should be assigned a function in the production. No job is too small. It is not the job that is small, it is the responsibility that is brought into discharging it that could be small. Give your training during the class training sessions, but give guidance during production sessions. Allow the talent to develop with some originality and ingenuity whether as actor, or stage designer or stage technician. Remember that the stage is a practical formative workshop for all disciplines. So give each student a chance to discover himself/herself. As we have said earlier, the production business offers the students guided learning as actors, designers, and technicians. And you, as the director, are the guide. Your job is enormous, but satisfying when a good effort goes down well with the audience.

Conclusion

This book does not pretend to be comprehensive as a guide to a drama student on acting. What it takes to go on stage cannot be fully documented in one book. We are confident however that if you follow what we have said so far and remain conscious of them at all times then you will be better equipped not only to work on stage, but also to appreciate plays and those engaged in producing them with greater understanding. After all, not all students who study drama will have the opportunity or desire to make a career or hobby of it. Our hope is that all students will eventually appreciate the values of going to the theatre regularly as part of their mental and social growth and also as part of their continuing intellectual enrichment. You will be a better member of the audience when you are knowledgeable about the industry that produced what you are witnessing. When you have the background knowledge you will be better equipped to be a critical and contemplative member of an audience.

We think it is befitting to conclude this book with the opinions of one of the world's greatest actors. His comments on acting are apt encouragement, advice and caution to all students of drama generally, but more applicable to those burning with ambition and dreams of becoming theatre luminaries. Lawrence Olivier is one of our twentieth century stag symbols. He has become world famous because of his star roles on stage (particularly in Shakespeare's plays) and in films. He has performed in the greatest theatres in the world. Stage has made him a very wealthy man. He is a happy man too. Married, he is still in love with his wife and takes interest in her own career. At over 70 years of age, he stands as a model and a father figure to growing actors all over the world.

Recently interviewed in Hollywood by *Times Magazine* (Dec.29, 1975) he had the following brief words to say about acting, and about his career on stage:

1. On Playing Parts: You see, the craft of the actor can be rewarding and happy. The basic inclination toward the work is to pretend to be or feel like someone else. You feel like a king, or you feel like an archbishop. That can be better than being a real king or a real churchman because they are stuck with that. Next month you, as an actor, can be somebody's uncle, and the month after that a Chairman, and that's an advantage. There are times when your life is suffused with bitterness and misery so that you can hardly endure to wear this particularly uncomfortable garment called life. I have been so wretched at times that I felt completely out of contact with reality. When I went on in a part in the night time, that was the only time I really felt like myself.

2. On Achieving Fame: I wanted it very much, but when I started playing leading parts in London, I wasn't popular at first. I swore to myself, "when I am popular I shall be so gracious to everybody. I will sit at the steps of the stage door saying. 'My people, how I love you. There are only 300 here? I can sign all the autographs. Some of you go off and have a drink, and then come back." But when I

became popular, I wasn't like that at all. I'd take one horrified look at them, turn up my coat collar and run.

3. On Drink As the Actor's Bane: It's a dreadful temptation. You see, one is sitting there in that dressing room from 6 to 8 with absolutely nothing to do, except possibly fret. And so actors begin drinking. And they drink during the play and they drink after the play. Years and years ago Ralphie (Richardson) and I made a mutual pact. We promised each other not to drink until the curtain went down and we kept that pact.

4. On relying on Flashes of Genius: I have always distrusted genius in my world. I won't tolerate that word applied to me because I don't believe in it. Genius for hard work, sure, sure. Genius for application. But the rest is gift, gift, gift, talent with luck, and ultimately, most important of all, skill.

5. On Fitness as to Craft, Health and Life: Breath control is essential. I tried to persuade old Charles Langhton* of that when he told me he was going to do Lear. He asked if I could give him any advice. I said, "Yes I can, you fat, old s.o.b. You have a large estate in Norfolk. I've seen it, not that you ever invited me to it, dear boy, I was catty. You have a large estate with an extensive hillside. Every morning I want you to climb that hillside, and shout out the lines." Well, he didn't do that, and he was absolutely no good.

When I was rehearsing for King Lear, I went on neighbouring land and I screamed King Lear at the cows, who all came up and thought it was marvellous. And I roared at them and they'd moo. But the point was to exercise the bellows. Just to go on and think, "oh, well, other people have done it, so I can," without preparing your whole physique for it, is a failure to realise that the basic need for being good at anything is to be in a fit condition for it. What you must finally achieve is the

---

* Another celebrated British actor.

proper initial humility toward the work and the difficult equation of the necessary confidence to carry it out. What you can do, you must do.

Index

www.ingramcontent.com/pod-product-compliance
Lightning Source LLC
Chambersburg PA
CBHW011509100726
47900CB00009B/2663